MW01205368

LAUNCH! THE GUIDE TO START YOUR OWN BUSINESS

An Illustrated Workbook to Create
a Profitable Side-Hustle (from Scratch!)

INTRODUCTION

How a simple idea with the right amount of attention can build you a sustainable income, even in hard times.

INTRODUCTION

There's an old saying that to escape a labyrinth you should turn left at every crossroads.

If only life were that simple.

In today's world, we're faced with all sorts of insidious 'labyrinths' that present us with an overwhelming paradox of choice. Do you stay at the job you hate or do you risk it all and start a new business? Do you take out a massive student loan and hope that you'll get an advantageous starting salary when you graduate, or do you skip school altogether and work your way up the ladder through hustle and self-education?

Whatever paths you originated from in your journey through the labyrinth, the fact that you picked up this book means you're facing the crossroad to 'start your own business' or not.

In the classic Greek myth of Theseus and the Minotaur, Theseus is sent to slay the Minotaur in the labyrinth. To help him find his way out after he completed the task, he was given a golden thread by a princess named Ariadne. The thread would be his guide to escape the labyrinth.

Now, I am no princess, but I did write this book to serve as a metaphorical golden thread to help you find your way out of the labyrinth.

Maybe the Minotaur in your story is a boss or a job you dread, maybe it's fear that you're not good enough, or perhaps it's a tall stack of bills. The labyrinth ahead of you might represent the complexity and risk involved in slaying your Minotaur, starting your business, and finding freedom at the end. This book will be your guide to accomplishing all of this, and help you avoid the pitfalls and wrong turns along the way. (Trust me, I faced a lot of those on my own journey through the labyrinth.) I've distilled the years of my experience starting different side hustles and put in a massive amount of effort to simplify these experiences into actionable, digestible exercises that will get you from the crossroads of starting, to running a thriving business as quickly as possible.

—

The 2020 pandemic might be the biggest crisis we have faced in our lifetime. It's also given us a glimpse into the importance of having a backup plan, a side hustle, a ready-to-deploy new income stream. Millions of people were thrown out of work overnight with the pandemic. And as our economy slowly rebuilds at the time of writing this, it's inspiring to see the ingenuity of many of my friends and acquaintances starting new side hustles.

Maybe you lost the ability to work in your industry, or maybe you got a salary cut and are looking for ways to add more income. Or maybe you're just not making enough cash at your main job and are looking for a way to be your own boss. Whatever the case, you're here because you want to bring more income into your life through your own means. Instead of working hard to build someone else's dreams, or burn yourself out getting paid less than you're worth at a job you don't care about, it's time you finally take things into your own hands and create a side hustle that can generate a healthy, consistent income you can scale quickly.

I wrote this book because I wanted to help people bridge the gap from dreaming about launching a side hustle to actually having a thriving operation that not only pays the bills, but has the potential to scale to a full fledged enterprise.

At the very least, this book will help you discover a plan to rebuild your livelihood, launch a new passion project, or lay the groundwork to be your own boss. I have a feeling that you will do much more than that. I have a feeling that the strength you acquire through these lessons will enable you to do incredible feats that can change your trajectory and set you up for a life of abundance. But no pressure — we're taking this one step at a time and are starting with the basics.

Who am I to write this book?

How do I know this stuff? Because I've been there. I've been in your shoes. I made a lot of stubborn, borderline stupid choices in my 20s that left me broke, in debt and out of work. But through tenacity and a lot of persistence, I was able to build a business that not only paid the bills for our team, but also helped fund additional projects like a full length feature film. I was then able to parlay the skills I learned running that business to get an amazing job at a marketing agency working directly with marketing legend Eric Siu. Meanwhile, I am continuing to launch new and exciting side hustles from painting, to photography, to educational courses and even physical products.

I launched my production company in a time when I literally had about $15 to my name. I was able to rally a team together, and we started making short films for actors. We hustled. We over delivered on every shoot we did. We honed our craft, we built a brand. Before we knew it, it was time to move into an office. Business kept growing and we kept increasing profits year after year.

The lesson here is, even if you're down and out, there's a way to find a hustle that can change the game for you. Also, because I know how frustrating it can be to not know the next steps, I've created this book to help you sidestep a lot of the mistakes I made starting my first businesses and help you navigate towards a thriving, profitable business as fast as possible.

So with that said, let's get to work building your brand new income stream.

This book is designed to take you from no idea to an income generating side hustle in less than eight weeks. Depending on the type of business you choose, you might even be able to do this faster. Service based businesses can generate revenue practically overnight. Other product based businesses may potentially take longer.

The ideas that we generate will be SIMPLE and ACTIONABLE. By being decisive with our ideas and focusing exclusively on the ones that will get us to revenue the fastest, we'll eliminate the urge to try everything under the sun. Once your idea is up and running, you'll have plenty of time to explore other ideas. But for the next eight weeks, we'll choose **one** ship to sail out of these rocky waters together.

Our journey to income is split up into 6 sections:

1. Coming up with a bunch of ideas
2. Selecting your most viable option
3. Preparing for launch
4. Launching
5. Getting your first sales
6. Refining and polishing

Each lesson you'll be asked to do an exercise that will get you closer to success. These exercises are designed to make your side hustle grow — plain and simple. It can be intimidating without a roadmap, so this guide will give you a step-by-step plan to launch your business without meandering around lost and confused about which step to take next.

But don't worry. You're not going to fail.

You're going to figure this out. It might be hard, but you're going to get through this and come out stronger than ever before.

The first section of this book is all about creative thinking. It's taken me dozens of years of experimenting, researching, failing, and succeeding to discover these brainstorming frameworks. I've had to learn this stuff the hard way. I've taken on side projects that ended up as dead ends, I've poured countless hours into projects that were abandoned in the end. What I've learned through these twists and turns is this: it's much more effective to abandon a bad idea early and go all in on your best "viable" idea *as soon as possible*.

The brainstorming and selection process of the next chapters will set you up so that you'll choose an idea with a bright, promising future and make the next 30 days (and the years to come) extremely profitable.

Now it's important to mention this: You're smart, and I know you'll figure this stuff out on your own eventually. That being said, we don't have the luxury to figure it out the hard way. In each lesson, I'm giving you some prompts to accelerate the process.

By the end of Part 1, you'll have brainstormed several ideas that can start to generate income FAST. This process should take you between two to seven days, and these first lessons can be done in under an hour each.

By the end of Part 2, you'll have made a research backed decision on your favorite idea and calculated your projected earnings. You'll have evaluated your ideas based on their long-term potential and scored them against each other. Finally, you'll have made a decision for which idea you'll run with through the rest of the book. This process should only take a few days and each lesson can be done in under an hour.

From Part 3 to 5, you'll be setting yourself up for a successful launch. From there, if you continue to put in one or two hours a day into doing the exercises in each lesson, you'll be making your first sale within 30 days from now.

Part 6 is designed to set you up for lasting success by providing a strong foundation and operating system for your business. Although the lessons from Part 6 are foundational and the action items can be completed in a few days, they are meant to be a lasting part of your future business journey. You will want to come back to these chapters as you continue to grow your business.

So, if you're ready to change your life, and start making income on your own, let's begin the journey!

Contents

PART 1

COMING UP WITH YOUR INCOME IDEAS

In the next few lessons, we'll dive deep into your passions, skills, callings, relationships, and resources to choose candidates for your new source of reliable cash flow.

This first section of the book is split into six lessons and exercises:

1. **Clear thinking and focus:** You will need to make a commitment to take your new side hustle seriously if you want it to succeed.
2. **You've got options:** There are many different ways to bring home the bacon, whether you're starting with products or services. This chapter will get the wheels spinning into what's possible for your first steps.
3. **Your skill and passion inventory:** We'll get creative and think of all the things you can possibly do.
4. **Effort can replace capital (most of the time):** Whether you're sitting on a nest egg ready to invest in your new idea or if you're working part-time living paycheck to paycheck, this chapter will give you clues on the kinds of businesses that will work best for your budget.
5. **Getting clear on your business idea:** How to distill your idea down to a simple, clear offering.
6. **Estimating the earning potential of your ideas:** This thing's gotta make money, right?

LESSON 1:
THINK OPPORTUNITY

LESSON 1

I KNOW YOU'RE EAGER TO GO OUT THERE AND START SELLING THINGS AND COLLECTING INVOICES ALREADY.

BUT BEFORE WE CAN EVEN THINK ABOUT WHAT BUSINESS YOU'RE GOING TO BE STARTING, WE NEED TO MAKE SPACE IN YOUR MIND FOR THE GOOD IDEAS.

RIGHT NOW, YOU MIGHT BE FEELING NERVOUS, OR PANICKED ABOUT GETTING YOUR PROJECT OFF THE GROUND...

...AND THAT'S TOTALLY UNDERSTANDABLE.

BUT IF YOUR BRAIN IS GOING WILD THINKING ABOUT ALL THE THINGS YOU'RE MISSING,

#!!@$??

YOU'RE NOT GIVING YOURSELF THE PERMISSION TO SEE THE OPPORTUNITIES YOU'RE SITTING ON.

AS YOGI BERRA SAYS, 90% OF THE GAME IS MENTAL, THE OTHER 10% IS PHYSICAL

FOR THE NEXT 30 DAYS, AS YOU START YOUR NEW BUSINESS, I'M ASKING YOU TO IMPLEMENT 3 PRACTICES DAILY

THAT WILL GIVE YOU AN INSANE MENTAL ADVANTAGE AND HELP YOU BREAK THROUGH ANY OBSTACLE YOU'LL FACE

NUMBER ONE

STOP DOUBTING YOURSELF. IN FACT, TELL YOURSELF OUT LOUD HOW INCREDIBLE YOU ARE EVERY SINGLE DAY, EVEN IF YOU DON'T "FEEL" IT.

NUMBER TWO

I AM CONFIDENT!

REMIND YOURSELF OF THE REASON YOU'RE DOING THIS. WHAT IS THE NORTH STAR THAT GUIDES YOU?

YOU NEED YOUR CONFIDENCE IF YOU'RE GOING TO BE ABLE TO TAKE RISKS AND PUT YOURSELF OUT THERE.

DRAFT A BRIEF VISION OF WHAT YOU WANT TO ACHIEVE BY STARTING A BUSINESS.

LESSON 1 DETAILS

TIMELINE: DAY ONE
ESTIMATED TIME TO COMPLETE: 30 MIN.

As we start on our great big adventure building a new side hustle, the most important thing you can do now is clear your mind of any panic or desperation and instead keep confident.

I decided to include this as the very first chapter of the book because it will lay the foundation for everything we do moving forward. As we make our first major decision for the type of side hustle you will be building in this book, we want that decision to be made from a calm, secure frame of mind. The first step is giving yourself the permission to believe that you can create an incredible, money generating side hustle that brings you joy. From there, we can begin to remove any doubt from your mind and let your most exciting and profitable ideas bubble to the surface.

We will do this through three distinct steps:

1. Stop doubting yourself. It is entirely possible to have new income. This book and your actions can even get you there in eight weeks or less.
2. Make a commitment to eliminate distractions and choose to focus on the path of building this business. You only have to commit to this until you get things up and running, then you can go back to whatever it was you were doing before (if you really want to).
3. Make a commitment to practicing some form of exercise and meditation. These will be critical in anchoring your new commitment to some immediately gratifying rewards, as well as boost your mental clarity and confidence.

Let's turn the clock back to a couple years before I started writing this book. I was going through a tough time emotionally. I couldn't find my edge. I felt like I had hit a plateau and was overwhelmed by self judgement and depression. I eventually decided enough was enough and I hired a coach, Dennis Procopio, to help me through it. He works with his clients guiding them through three distinct stages of growth spread across a 12 month program: the Survival Phase, the Maintenance Phase, and the Creation Phase.

When I started working with him, I was definitely in the survival phase. Things were unraveling all around me. Relationships were falling apart, my finances were shaky, and I was on the edge of losing my job. The good news is, with a lot of discipline and positive thinking I was able to turn everything around and launch myself all the way to the creative phase. This book is a testament to that.

Now, let's bring it back to you. Maybe you're smack dab in the middle of the survival phase right now, or maybe things are going pretty well in your life and you're simply looking to start a new side hustle. In either case, going back to the basics to hone your positive thinking and discipline will always come in handy.

The reason we're starting the book off talking about exercise and meditation is because of one very real truth: starting a new business will be hard. It will be especially hard if you're doing this as a side hustle while still working a full time job or managing a household. You will need your mind and body sharp so you don't run out of energy, motivation, or faith in yourself. Taking care of your body will keep your confidence at its peak and will help you push through whatever challenges show up along the way.

The thing is, you're here because you want to make a change and start something incredible. Changing from survival mode to creative mode is going to take some discipline, but don't worry, this guide will give you each step along the way. All you have to do is make sure you set aside the time each day to do the exercises and keep making progress.

Your new business, and your future self depend on you sticking through with this mission. You can't get sidetracked by scrolling through your social media to read the latest meme or watch TikTok skits.

You'll need to be disciplined and focused. You'll need to roll your sleeves up and do the kind of work you never had to do before. Times are different. Times are harder. But you got this. You're going to use this as an opportunity to grow, to build a foundation so strong that no one can stop you. But most of all, you'll be having fun along the way, because you're now living life on YOUR terms.

For today, the game plan is to start earnestly thinking about things that you can try that can become a reliable source of income. The one thing that we're going to avoid is being critical of either your capabilities or your ideas. You have tons of potential — and we will undoubtedly come up with several viable ideas so you can pick and choose the one you resonate the most with.

It's time to begin thinking with a mindset of possibilities and potential. There's no need to think about any reasons why we'll fail, or to be preoccupied with any kind of fear or doubt. Who cares what other people say or think? I believe in you. I know you can do this. I want you to simply start believing in yourself, too.

So part one of today's mission is to simply start thinking POSITIVELY — you can achieve anything. That's the kind of mindset we're approaching this with. The weeks ahead present us with a blank slate that you will write your future on. Part of our mission is to get you an extra stream of reliable side income, but along the way, we'll build a ton of valuable skills that you can take with you in all your future endeavors.

Let's get back to regular exercise and meditation.

According to the article[1] from Harvard, exercise 'has a unique capacity to exhilarate and relax, to provide stimulation and calm, to counter depression and dissipate stress.' The article goes on to explain how meditation does the same. You KNOW this stuff is good for you, so I'm not going to waste much more time trying to convince you about the merits of exercise — there's a dozen YouTube channels like Ben Greenfield Fitness that can do that job. The point is, if there is any time where you should start these activities, it's now.

Starting your new business is going to stretch your limits mentally and physically. Let exercise and meditation be a daily practice in your life throughout the duration of this program and you'll be better equipped to weather the increased challenge. I don't care how many minutes each day you do them for. I just want your commitment that you'll apply some form of quiet thinking and movement in your routine for the coming weeks.

Beyond that, your best ideas will come to you when you make space in your mind for them. Exercise keeps the negative thoughts at bay, meditation keeps you focused and clear headed.

Personally, I enjoy doing a kinetic meditation, where I sit with a pen and paper and slowly make random dots on the page for half an hour. You can do

---

1   https://www.health.harvard.edu/staying-healthy/exercising-to-relax

a walking meditation or just quietly sit on a fluffy pillow. Whatever. Simply give yourself the time and space to clear your mind, and do your preferred form of meditation. No negotiations here. You don't have the luxury to skip this. A clear mind will be your greatest ally in these challenging times.

Build a habit around exercise and meditation. We'll need you at top form mentally and physically during this program. This is your fundamental exercise. If you're already doing this as part of your routine, great, you can move on to Lesson 2.

If you haven't started exercising or meditating yet — do it before moving on to Lesson 2. That means go for a walk, sit in a chair and clear your mind for 10, 20, or even 30 minutes — whatever you need to feel a little more peaceful. Then, when you're ready, grab a pen and paper and we'll move on to Lesson 2.

SUMMARY OF THIS LESSON'S ACTION ITEMS:

- Clear your mind and start thinking about your new life making money doing a new side business.
- Think opportunity and positivity — don't think about fears.
- Make a commitment to practice some form of meditation and exercise.
- Finally, make a commitment to put aside or limit your access to distractions and trivial activities for the next 30 days. This means limiting your time on social media, streaming services, video games, dating, social drinking, etc.

TIP:

Every time you make a choice to scroll through Instagram or TikTok, you're pulling yourself away from your dreams. If you have to, delete the apps from your phone for eight weeks. Don't worry, you can reinstall them after the program (if you want to). You were able to do social distancing during the pandemic, you can do this.

It might be difficult to pull yourself away from a habit like this. One thing that tends to work really well is replacing the habit with a similar experience. If you're addicted to scrolling social media, try to replace that activity with something like solving Sudoku puzzles on your phone instead. Every time you get the urge to scroll social media, Sudoku will be there to satisfy the urge in a more healthy experience. You can learn more about habits and how to change them from James Clear's blog at www.jamesclear.com.

LESSON 2: SERVICE BUSINESS VS. PRODUCTS BUSINESS

LESSON 2 DETAILS

TIMELINE: DAY TWO
ESTIMATED TIME TO COMPLETE: 15 MIN.

In the coming lessons, we'll begin coming up with some fun ideas along with ways for those ideas to make money. We'll want to think about all the possible options you have on the table. From there, you can make a choice that aligns best with your experience, goals, and cash on hand.

As we get ready to start the idea generation process, let's set the stage by going over what type of businesses you can actually start with. This lesson will give you an understanding of how to categorize each of your ideas as either a service based business or a products based business.

Generally speaking, most businesses will fall into one of these two categories: either you're collecting money in exchange for a product (examples: ebooks, handcrafted bath products, or vintage guitars) or you're exchanging money for a service rendered (examples: dog washing, lawn care, or digital marketing account management). Yes, there are ways to turn a service into a product, but we'll get into that later when we talk about scaling.

To have a business you have to sell something. However, that "something" can be almost anything. Remember, the mission in this book is to launch your new venture as quickly as possible. So, naturally we'll want to select a path that has both a clear ability to start generating money quickly and has potential to grow exponentially in the long term.

A service business gives you the ability to jump in and start trading your time and expertise for payment practically right away. If you're creative and use the lessons in this book to market your service well, you should have no problem transforming your free time and effort into a cash generating machine. On the other hand, a product business gives you the opportunity to multiply your time and sell your "something" to many people simultaneously. The challenge with products is that they take a lot more time, energy, and cash up front to build.

Some of you are in a better position to get things rolling with a service business, while others are ready for a product. We're all coming from different starting points, so as you read about the different advantages of each type of business, think about which will be best suited for your individual needs.

As a broad generalization, services are easier to start and grow in the early stages. Products can be more profitable in the long run, but are more difficult and costly to launch out of the gate. There are always exceptions, of course.

Three basic factors play into whether you eventually start a service or products business: your level of interest, any pre-existing skills or abilities, and your long term goals. For example, if you are a skilled graphic designer already, it makes sense to start a service-oriented business selling design work. If you love tech gadgets or garden decorations, a business that sells those products will keep you interested.

Naturally, your end goal is important too. You don't need to decide which path you take until Lesson Seven, but this foundational chapter will help you make an informed decision. One important thing to keep in mind as you move forward with this book is that I strongly advise against starting a business with debt or by seeking investors. With the tools and strategies outlined in this book, you should be able to start generating consistent income with your business and can work up to that big, expensive idea later.

Pros of a service business:

- You can literally start today. You simply need to present your service to a buyer and collect payment.
- Sites like Fiverr, Upwork, and Yelp can give you access to buyers all over the world or in your neighborhood.
- You can grow a service business by simply adding more clients and adding more talented people to your team.
- You can raise your prices as you develop a reputation and your skill level increases.

Cons of a service business:

- You are effectively trading your time for money. Finishing jobs for clients may take hours or days and this is time you can't earn money from another client.
- You may encounter lots of competition. The barriers to entry are low in a service business, so you'll have to be remarkable to stand out.

Pros of a product business:

- You're able to sell to multiple customers at the same time.
- Your revenue can grow exponentially, regardless of how many employees you have.
- You can boost your profits as you grow by making your entire operation more efficient.

Cons of a product business:

- It takes a long time to build your prototypes, set up distribution channels, and create your marketing plan.
- Products can easily become very expensive. You will need to invest more capital upfront to set everything up.
- Products are hard. If you don't know how to source affordable materials or set up distribution logistics (shipping, returns, etc.) already you'll have a lot of research and studying ahead of you.

In light of all these ideas, there's also some nontraditional methods available. If you don't have the capital at hand to invest in your own manufacturing or the space to keep inventory, drop shipping or selling digital products can give you a less risky means to get started with products. Drop shipping means selling another company's products in your own shop but letting the manufacturer handle all the logistics. All you are responsible for is the marketing. Digital products are simple to deliver via email or file sharing services online and can be things like online courses, ebooks, or webinars.

Examples of service and product business ideas

Service Businesses

- Freelance work (graphic design, writing, web development, editing)
- Online assistance (virtual admin, consulting, tutoring, marketing help)
- Real-world services (plumbing, lawn mowing, music lessons, house organizing, etc.)
- Coaching and consulting (fitness, nutrition, mental wellness, business or executive training)
- Agency style services (full-stack web development, architecture, marketing, animation studios)
- Mobile services (massage therapy, pet grooming, office or home cleaning)

Product Businesses

- Selling personal items (online auctions, social media marketplaces, used goods)
- Drop shipping (marketing other companies' products without inventory)
- Digital products (stock photos or graphics, online courses, print on demand products)
- Art or craft sales (takes time to create inventory, custom commissions)
- Physical products that you manufacture (fashion products, jewelry, home goods, crafts)
- Book sales (time to write, formatting, design, and professional editing investments).

SUMMARY OF THIS LESSON'S ACTION ITEMS:

- Take a few minutes to think about the concepts of service businesses versus products businesses and some examples that you've seen out there in the wild. In the next chapter, we'll begin brainstorming an arsenal of ideas that you can turn into side hustles. It will be helpful to have this understanding of the pros and cons of these two key types of businesses so that you can steer your brainstorming session to the style that suits you best.

LESSON 3:
BRAINSTORM
A BUNCH OF IDEAS

WITH A LITTLE OUT OF THE BOX THINKING, WE'LL BE ABLE TO COME UP WITH SEVERAL GREAT IDEAS.

THE SIMPLE FRAMEWORKS IN THIS SECTION WILL TAKE THE BURDEN OUT OF BRAINSTORMING IDEAS

SO YOU CAN CONFIDENTLY JUMP RIGHT INTO YOUR NEXT SIDE HUSTLE WITHOUT FEELING LIKE YOU MADE A WRONG TURN.

YOUR MISSION

USE THE BRAINSTORMING METHODS ON THE NEXT PAGE TO COME UP WITH AT LEAST 3 — IDEALLY 5 — POTENTIAL IDEAS FOR YOUR NEXT BUSINESS.

IN THE NEXT SECTION, WE'LL EVALUATE AND SCORE THE IDEAS BEFORE SELECTING THE WINNER, SO GO GET CREATIVE AND HAVE FUN WITH THIS EXERCISE!

LESSON 3 DETAILS

One of the reasons I hear so frequently for people giving up on starting a side hustle is not being able to come up with a "good" idea. This lesson is designed to help get you out of the trap of thinking that you don't have any worthwhile ideas, and give you a proactive approach to discover ideas in places you least expected.

Because I know that you are an amazing, talented, creative person, I have no doubt that you have a great many possibilities just waiting to be discovered. Now, today, you're going to draw from your unique experiences, adventures, skills, and even your individual desires to find some ideas that can be further elaborated on in the next lessons.

What I want to encourage you to try in this lesson is to keep a nonjudgmental attitude towards the ideas you come up with. We're encouraging imagination and exploration in this lesson, and if we stop this exploration to critique the ideas we're coming up with, it might hold us back from our most creative ideas. Imagination and creativity can sometimes manifest like a shy rabbit, timidly revealing itself from the concealing bushes of our mind only when it feels safe and free from judgement.

Brainstorm Method 1: Your Experience Inventory

Look for ideas based on your skills, interests, other people's ideas, and things around the world that you could make better.

Here are four places you are likely to find some great ideas for profitable side hustles:

1. Your hobbies and interests

    - *Example*: Noelle has a lot of friends that are entertainers. She connects talented entertainment providers with people hosting parties (bat mitzvahs, weddings, etc.) and takes a booking fee.

2. Your special skill sets, knowledge, or expertise

    - *Example*: John is a talented chef with a great personality. He makes cooking videos, sells meal prep guides, and earns affiliate commissions when people buy the products he recommends.
    - *Example*: Jesse makes hand crafted barbeque tools and sells them online and at local farmers markets.
    - *Example*: Brianne loves acting and filmmaking. She made an online course teaching actors how to earn money on the side as a voiceover actor.

3. Copying/Borrowing/Stealing ideas from existing business models

    - There are a ton of business models out there that you can take and put your own spin on to start generating income. Here are a few that you can swipe and deploy to your heart's content:
        - › Learn how to do drop shipping and earn commission selling other people's products.
        - › Become a freelancer and do services like web design, photography, marketing, or even gardening. (You can list your service on sites like Fiverr, TaskRabbit, Upwork, Thumbtack, Yelp, etc.)
        - › Start a podcast and earn money through advertising, infoproducts, or memberships.
        - › Create an online course where you teach people how to do something you're really good at.

- ➤ Make a YouTube channel and earn affiliate commissions from the products you recommend on the show.
- ➤ Offer your expertise as a consultant.
- ➤ Create and sell meal prep guides, nutrition guides, or a recipe book.
- ➤ Offer writing services or proofreading services.
- ➤ Sell handcrafted goods or art on Etsy, Ebay or Amazon Handmade.
- ➤ Create a mastermind or membership group and charge for access.
- ➤ Write a blog or a website that focuses on a niche topic with daily content and earn revenue through sponsors, affiliates, or advertising.
- ➤ Use sites like Faire or Alibaba to buy wholesale products and resell with a profit.
- ➤ Create a subscription box with a collection of curated goods around a niche.
- ➤ Host paid events or seminars (these can even be virtual if you're stuck at home).
- ➤ Write and self publish a book on Amazon.
- ➤ Create a comic book and earn money through selling advertising and merchandise.
- ➤ Start a social media management agency.

4. Inefficiencies/Frustrations you see in the world around you

- These are the things that you see around the world that you wish "someone" would fix. Now that you're looking through the lens of opportunity, these roadblocks will begin to appear as opportunities that you can solve.
- *Example*: Maybe you got frustrated because there was no toilet paper at the store when the COVID-19 pandemic happened, so you decided to start a toilet paper subscription box. Your customers could always count on having fresh TP delivered to their doorstep, even in hard times.

If your Experience Inventory ideas are still not what you're looking for, or you're just coming up short on ideas, you can try these additional brainstorming methods to come up with some very powerful ideas.

Brainstorm Method 2: The Ikigai Matrix

Ikigai is a Japanese word that means "life calling." The concept is simple: we're looking for a central purpose that fulfills as many areas of life as possible.

Write 4 columns on a paper. Title each column as follows:

1. Things I'm SKILLED at
2. Things I SHOULD be doing (i.e. what the world needs)
3. Things I can get PAID for doing
4. Things I LOVE to do

Next, write seven to ten things in each column. It doesn't matter how wacky or selfish these are. If you like wearing clown suits or can get paid for playing backgammon, put that in there — no shame!

Once you have AT LEAST seven in each category, start to look for commonalities. If you have the same entry in four columns, you've found something that can be your "calling" or Ikigai. Bring that idea to the next step.

You might also find a couple other ideas that fit in two or three columns that will be more feasible than an idea that fits all columns. Bring these ideas to the next round as well.

Brainstorming Method 3: Get some exercise

You've probably heard this from a lot of credible sources — some of the best ideas come from doing moderate exercise. Get out and go for a jog, hike in nature, swim in the ocean, run on the treadmill. You'll not only feel great, but the exercise will get your brain moving and shake in some fresh perspective.

Brainstorm Method 4: Contact me or another trusted mentor for a strategy call

If you're hitting a wall and don't feel like your ideas are "right," visit my website www.startbrigade.com and schedule a strategy call. I also have a community you can join where you can get advice from other hustlers like yourself.

Now, once you have your list of potential ideas, we'll bring them to the next section where we weigh out the pros and cons — and start bringing them to life.

Here's the catch: your idea should be something that you can start without a major capital investment or business loan. You want to have a stream of income that is entirely your own. You don't want to start things off with a debt. More on this in the next section!

SUMMARY OF THIS LESSON'S ACTION ITEMS:

- Sit down with a pad of paper, a good pen, and an open mind. Make sure you have removed yourself from distractions and get ready to dive into the four brainstorming methods below until you have about five to seven ideas you can see yourself realistically doing.
- Go through your experience inventory noting the special skills that you think you can turn into a business or cool business models you've seen other people launching. You can also shop through the examples I've mentioned above. Get creative and challenge yourself to put a few ideas you might not normally consider in the list.
- If you're in need of some additional deep brainstorming, try using the Ikigai method to find the sweet spot of side hustles that you enjoy, are skilled at, can get paid for, and feel you should be doing out of moral or civic responsibility.
- If your list still looks sparse after this, go get some exercise to clear your mind, or schedule a strategy call with me or another mentor.

TIP:

If you want a killer tool that can take your brainstorming to the next level, visit StarterStory.com This site has hundreds of case studies of everyday people just like you who took a chance with a business idea and made it happen. On the site there is an in-depth report of how each of these businesses got started, including how much capital they used to launch and how much revenue they earn.

Personally, I particularly enjoy the reports the site makes on the different types of business models and their respective pros and cons.

You can simply browse through the hundreds of different business ideas until you find one that resonates with you, then adopt that business model for yourself. The remaining lessons in this book will give you a framework to make your version unique as well as successful.

LESSON 4:
NO MONEY DOWN
VS. INVESTING AT
THE START

LESSON 4 DETAILS

You're going to have to spend some money to launch a side hustle, a business, or even a hobby. Although there's not a whole lot of wiggle room here, there are certainly ways to start a business for cheap.

As a disclaimer, spending money on a new business should really only happen after considerable research into your probable return on investment. Of course, you don't need to have a trust fund to launch a business. Bootstrapping with only a small amount of personal funds can still bring you life-changing results.

People from all different walks of life and personal circumstances can improve their position by starting their own business. Some common starting circumstances might be:

- You have saved money to invest in your new business. You are ready to take a risk but are still not sure you have the right idea or know-how to succeed.
- You have money but feel completely lost when it comes to taking action to create an income-producing venture.
- You lack money but you have marketable skills, experience, and credibility in your field.
- You don't want to risk much money, but you have a lot of time and willingness to put in as much effort as it takes to succeed.
- You have little to no extra money, but you have plenty of extra time and a strong passion to both learn new marketable skills and out-hustle the folks with cash in their pockets.

Do you see yourself in any of these examples? Maybe you have different circumstances entirely. I have tried to create this book for most aspiring business owners. You can succeed if you think creatively about how to align your skills and resources with people who will want to pay for them.

Plenty of options exist. Even if you're starting small, it's important to think about how the business you create today can become fuel for greater endeavors down the road. That's the beauty of bootstrapping: you're able to generate cash flow with your first business that you can deploy later. This is a concept that Andrew Wilkinson of Tiny Capital calls the "Launch Pad Business" concept.

You can build a modest, reliable platform with enough cash flow that will help you reach loftier heights in the future. A 'launch pad business' works exactly like that. Any service or product business can become a launch pad for something even greater. Before you worry about leveraging profits and scaling your entire venture, you need to create a simple foundation that works.

If you're short on cash or cannot take the risk due to your personal financial situation, don't worry. Roll up your sleeves, dig in, learn a lot, and choose a product or service business that works with time, know-how, and effort. Throughout this book, I will share more examples and ideas that will help you find success whichever path you choose.

In this lesson, your assignment is to simply take a look at your current cash situation and decide how much you're comfortable with investing in your business. You can also do some rearranging of your expenses and figure out ways to cut unnecessary costs that you can otherwise invest into growing your business.

Maybe you're eating out for lunch every day instead of prepping your meals at home. Depending on where you live, that can easily add up to $400 or more in savings that you can instead invest in your business. So take a few minutes to look at your finances and make a note about your realistic ability to invest in your business.

SUMMARY OF THIS LESSON'S ACTION ITEMS:

- Take some time to think about what a bootstrapped version of your business can look like. How lean and simple can you start with? Once your business is starting to generate income you can begin to use that income to expand it, or start the next venture.
- Do some serious thinking about how much you are willing to invest into your business. We'll use the next chapter to start calculating how much money you can earn from the different types of businesses, so for now, simply calculate what you're able to invest.

TIP:

The best time to plant a tree is ten years ago. The second best time is right now. It takes a lot of guts to start a side hustle. I know people who have been on the edge of the starting line for many years, waiting for the 'perfect' time. The perfect time doesn't really ever show up. It's always been there, waiting for you to gather enough courage to make the first step.

So no pressure! You got this. Whether you're sitting on a nest egg or making ends meet with a day job while you chip away at your new side hustle, the progress you'll make by starting today will be something you can be proud of years from now.

LESSON 5: DEVELOP THE IDEAS THAT SOUND PROMISING

NOT ALL IDEAS . . .

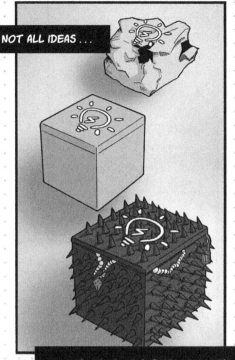

. . . ARE CREATED EQUAL

LESSON 5

THINK OF YOUR BUSINESS IDEAS LIKE QUESTS IN A VIDEO GAME:

LOW DIFFICULTY

SOME IDEAS ARE SAFE . . .

. . . BUT THEY WON'T EARN YOU MUCH MONEY OR EXPERIENCE.

LESSON 5 DETAILS

By now you should have a list of several potential projects, or breadcrumbs, that might turn into an idea with further exploration.

In this step, we'll go through what makes an idea a potential candidate for our idea arena, and what ideas get abandoned or postponed until the time is right.

Being able to be decisive here is critical. You can't afford to waste your time deliberating about a fantasy that's too unrealistic to achieve. Write those fantasies down and put them in a vault that you can go explore when you have a bunch of free time and extra capital. Trust me, you are not losing ANYTHING by letting go of your "wouldn't it be cool if" ideas for now. Let's focus on the "attainable in 30 days" kind of ideas.

Don't worry about evaluating if each idea is "perfect" — we'll dive into that later.

Qualities of a good idea

1. Can be achieved in 30 days or less
2. Doesn't require more capital or investment than you can afford right now
3. You can start making money right away
4. Is simple enough that you can describe it to your grandmother in 30 seconds (and she'll understand it)
5. Has the potential to be scaled — meaning you're not simply doing an hourly "job"

Qualities of an idea to forget about

1. You need to invest months into building the idea
2. You need funding
3. You won't earn income from it for a long time (30 days +)
4. It's hard to explain
5. You're trading your time for money — stuck in a "job"

Out of these ideas, pick at least 3 that you can potentially turn into a business. You should be able to clearly write what kind of product or service it is, and who would be purchasing it. Don't worry about going into specifics just yet.

Turn the idea into a simple 3 sentence description.

1. What is it?
2. Who will be the customer?
3. How does it make money?

An example for this might be:

1. **What:** Step by step meal prep plans, recipes and Instacart shopping lists delivered in a weekly newsletter.
2. **Who:** People who are affected by the recession, not able to eat out as much and are looking for tasty options they can cook at home while saving money
3. **How does it make money:** There will be a small subscription fee for the newsletter ($5/month) and additional affiliate revenue through promoting appliances and related brands.

To bring this full circle with Lesson 4: it might sound really tempting to build an app that can be the next big thing, but that's not our mission right now. Let's think about things that have earning potential right away. Things you can bootstrap with a little elbow grease and maybe some very minimal investment.

Additionally, I won't get into partnerships or investments in this book. That's a different problem for a different time. Our mission is to fill your immediate need for income. There are special cases where partnerships can work out, but let's get your new cashflow business up and running before worrying about some world changing new app idea.

SUMMARY OF THIS LESSON'S ACTION ITEMS:

- Go through all the ideas you came up with and evaluate them as either an idea to pursue in the next 30 days, or an idea to put on the back burner for a distant future.
- Take your remaining viable ideas and simplify the concept down to three clear, succinct sentences that address the what, who, and how of each of your business ideas.

TIP:

You'll be able to achieve incredible clarity around each idea by writing a concise description of a concept. That being said, it's pretty challenging to construct one of these short, clear and compelling descriptions. Whenever you're faced with a task that seems really challenging, you can tackle it head on and practice it like a drill until you feel incredibly comfortable with that task.

Practice drills are going to be extremely helpful as you begin to explore a brand new frontier of tasks, projects and scenarios growing your business. In his book *Ultra Learning*, Scott Young provides a powerful framework for integrating drills into your learning practice. You can also read about it on his numerous blog posts by searching for '*Ultra Learning drills*' on Google.

The key concept here is you can identify components of tasks that you are weak in, and drill those weak points until you feel confident. Then repeat as you discover another weak point. If you struggled to write your clear descriptions of the different ideas, you can drill this task until it's easy by writing short descriptions for a bunch of existing businesses that you're already familiar with.

LESSON 6:
ESTIMATE EARNINGS

LESSON 6 DETAILS

In this lesson, I want to save you the excruciating pain of blindly believing so hard that your amazing idea would be the next big thing — only to realize three months later that you forgot to calculate how it would actually make money and are forced to dejectedly toss it in the dumpster and go back to square one.

I burned through so many projects in my 20s and 30s, investing my savings on silly ideas and quitting jobs to chase the shimmering mirage of a half baked business idea. Once in a while, I'd get things to work, and looking back, the thing that separated the wins from the devastating losses was one thing: a plan to earn revenue.

It's impossible to predict the future, but that doesn't mean you should charge forward without estimating your expenses and revenues. A good business is like a train on a set of tracks. The tracks are there so the train doesn't have to stop and guess which way to go along the trip. A solid plan will point your tracks in the right direction, and a solid budget will make sure you have enough track to actually reach your destination. So, before you send your train on its grand journey, you'll want to make sure you have enough track to reach the target destination.

At this stage, you're really only able to take a wild guess at whether the idea is going to work out financially, but you'd be surprised at how accurate a few numbers on the back of a napkin can actually be. By this point, you should have some basic level of understanding around the business or industry you're in, and with a little research, you should be able to figure out how your competitors are making money.

It's possible to predict whether or not your business idea will make any money without hiring a fortune teller or an accountant.

To do this, we'll simply estimate what an average month would look like once your business is up and running. We'll make estimates for the following elements:

- The number of orders you can successfully fulfill per month
- The price you charge for each order
- The cost of all the materials and outsourced labor to fulfill each order
- Any costs related to advertising or marketing to get your customer
- And of course, the cost for your overhead expenses each month

After you make estimates for these elements, you'll simply multiply the number of orders and the price of each order to find your revenue. Then you would subtract your total monthly costs from the monthly revenue to find your profit. If it sounds simple, good. It's supposed to be simple at this stage. You can go through a more detailed financial projection once you select your business idea and do some more in depth research.

You can use a simple table like the one below to calculate your revenue, expenses and profit:

Business Idea:

Number of orders	Price per order	Subtotal of revenue			Total monthly revenue

Number of orders	Costs per order	Subtotal of order costs	Marketing Costs (monthly)	Operating expenses (monthly)	Total monthly cost

			Total monthly profit

Let's walk through an example of how you can put this into practice. When I was starting a photography side hustle, I wanted to make sure I could earn a few extra bucks on the side, but not sacrifice the time I would need to spend on my day job or with my friends and family. So I estimated that I could realistically only commit to six photo sessions a month. I looked up what other photographers in the area were charging and decided I could reasonably charge for a typical headshot session at $300. That would bring my maximum monthly revenue to $1,800. Some months I might make more, others less.

Then I estimated the costs. Although there is a hefty startup cost for photography equipment, I could split it up across several months. Let's say for my studio overhead and equipment costs I would be investing about $300 each month. Additionally, every photo session, I would need to hire a photo retoucher to make the images look great. Let's estimate that cost at $50 per session. At six sessions a month, that would add up to a total of $300.

Finally, I would need to run some promotions to attract customers every month. I estimated it would cost about $50 to get a customer through running some paid promotions. So another $300 a month in total.

Wow. So after doing the numbers, my expenses were really starting to stack up. Each month I would be spending $900 and earning $1,800. That left me with a profit of $900 a month. Of course once you get the business up and running there are plenty of ways to cut down expenses and increase rates. I ended up spending much less in promotion once people started referring friends to me.

Photography Business

Number of orders	Price per order	Subtotal of revenue			Total monthly revenue
6	300	1800			1800

Number of orders	Costs per order	Subtotal of order costs	Marketing Costs (monthly)	Operating expenses (monthly)	Total monthly cost
6	50 (RETOUCHING)	300	300	300	900

	Total monthly profit	900

Let's run another couple examples in the chart. Jon loves cars and is thinking about starting a Turo business where he rents out two of his cars when he's not using them. For context, Turo is a car sharing marketplace. We'll fill in the chart based on Jon assuming he can get 30 rentals each month. He'll have some other expenses like washing the vehicles, commission fees to Turo, and a general maintenance cost. He'll also need to factor in car payments and any storage or parking fees each month. Let's calculate based on these estimates:

- 30 orders per month
- $70 average rental price
- $5 car wash per rental
- $21 commission fee per rental
- $5 general maintenance per rental
- $0 marketing expenses since Jon is relying on Turo to get customers
- $400 monthly car payment (at $200 per car)

Car Rental Business:

Number of orders	Price per order	Subtotal of revenue				Total monthly revenue
30	70	2100				2100

Number of orders	Costs per order	Subtotal of order costs	Marketing Costs (monthly)	Operating expenses (monthly)	Total monthly cost
30	31	930		400	1330

	Total monthly profit	770

Jon's Turo business looks like it has the potential to be relatively profitable as long as he keeps the orders up and maintains the vehicles with a positive rating on the Turo marketplace. It might not be earning him enough to quit a day job, but he is likely to be able to pay for the loan payments on his cars and still have a little cash left over.

Each of your ideas will have different estimated revenues, and some service based ideas will have a limit unless you can figure out a way to add more hours through hiring staff, or increase the sale price by improving the customer experience. In Jon's example, he can increase his earnings by adding more cars to his roster that are both in high demand and can attract a higher rental price.

> I'm going to stress this last point because it's crazy important: it can be very tempting to cook up some optimistic revenue numbers and brush potential costs under the rug because you have a subconscious desire to not kill an idea. If you notice yourself being swayed by an avoidance to objectively estimate the revenue, I strongly suggest getting some outside perspective from a peer or mentor.

SUMMARY OF THIS LESSON'S ACTION ITEMS:

- Go through each idea and estimate the basic costs, sale price and monthly order quantity for each different business.
- Tally up the totals for each business idea and see which ones have the potential to grow beyond a "time for money" type of business.

TIP:

Getting good at napkin math doesn't have to be hard. In fact the whole premise is supposed to be easy. There's a fascinating article on Wired[2] that talks about how the hardest part of napkin math is learning to simplify things and be okay with making approximations or estimates.

You'll be able to use this same style of making simple calculations later on in your business when it comes to decisions like whether you should spend on advertising or invest in hiring more service providers. If this is a skill you want to master, take a few minutes to practice some of the physics problems in the Wired article. They're fun.

---

2 https://www.wired.com/story/how-to-get-better-at-back-of-the-envelope-calculations/

PART 2
SELECTING YOUR
WINNING IDEA

Let's paint a scenario for you here. Imagine getting really excited about a particular idea. On paper everything looks amazing. You're passionate about the type of service, you anticipate making a decent profit with it, there's even room to scale when it takes off. The only problem is that you don't really know how you'll get your customers. You decide to run with the idea anyway, planning to figure it out in the next steps.

You build a website, you contact suppliers, you create the products and even arrange for some prototypes to be made so you can take photos to create promotional products. You spend a solid month of effort and a hefty chunk of cash building your store. It looks incredible. You even begin building content for the website so you can rank in search queries. You've been so busy building the shop that you've brushed the lingering question of how it makes money under the rug to avoid it, hoping it might solve itself in time. Everything's coming along nicely... until it comes time to get a sale.

After calculating the costs to attract your customer, and pay your contractors, you would be left with no profit. Stubbornly, you try to see if you can find another customer who will pay a higher price... and before you know it, the project is just not fun anymore.

Interestingly enough, this has been me several times. I would keep trucking down the rabbit hole, avoiding the signs that an idea wouldn't be profitable quickly, stubbornly asserting that I could find a way to make it pay off before my passion wore out.

The next few lessons will help you avoid my mistakes and allow you to zero in on an idea that will not only have the best potential for profit, but also be fun and enjoyable in the process.

This following section of the book is split into five lessons and exercises:

1. **Score your ideas**: How to make the decision between your possible candidates.
2. **Visualize your ideas at scale**: How to differentiate between an idea that can grow versus an idea that will become a 'job' for you.
3. **Imagining yourself living the idea out in the long run**: How to determine if you will grow to love the ideas or find your energy fizzle out as you grow the business.
4. **Picking a winner**: Yes, in this lesson we will choose your top business idea and get ready to run with it.
5. **Creating your rapid fire business plan**: A step-by-step worksheet to build the roadmap for your business over the next several months.

LESSON 7:
SCORE YOUR IDEAS

... YOUR ENTHUSIASM OR PASSION FOR THE IDEA ...

... THE FEASIBILITY OF THE IDEA ...

... AND FINALLY, WHETHER OR NOT THERE IS A DEMAND FOR THE IDEA CURRENTLY.

LESSON 7 DETAILS

So now that you've put in the work to come up with some really appealing ideas and have done some well thought out estimates of how profitable they can become, it's time to score them with a simple qualitative metric that can help you identify which of the ideas is the one you should go all in on. Your gut instinct is usually very strong, but we want to supplement that instinct with some qualitative data as well.

To complete this lesson, you'll score the ideas on a worksheet that calculates how difficult each idea is, how expensive it is, how realistic it is, and of course, how profitable it will be. This concept of idea validation is inspired from the work of Chris Guillebeau, who I consider the 'godfather' of side hustles. You can learn more about idea validation in several of his books, including my favorite: The $100 Startup.

The simple chart I like to use when evaluating a new idea looks like this:

Business Idea	Passion Level	Income Potential	Ease	Current Demand	Total Score
1.					
2.					
3.					

Score each block on a 1–10 with 10 being the most desirable/feasible and 1 being the least. Total them up at the end — the idea with the highest score is your winner.

Your Passion Level: How much do you enjoy doing this? You'll need to be self motivated to power through and build this even when you're tired. Of course, the things that you might really enjoy doing might not have income potential, so we're looking for an idea that you can still enjoy enough to be motivated about it, but it can still make money.

Income Potential: Be realistic. What would you pay for this idea if you were a customer? What are people paying for this type of idea now? How many sales can you fulfill at what selling price? Can this idea be scaled quickly?

Ease of Implementation: Is this as easy as flipping a switch and signing up for driving Uber? Do you need to build prototypes? Do you need to write a book or film a course? Are there legal or lifestyle restrictions to this idea? This should also include any upfront costs that the project will likely demand.

Current Market Demand: Don't underestimate this section. This is the difference between a successful, income generating idea and a fun experience. I've dabbled in a BUNCH of ideas that no one really needed. Yes, there are people out there who might buy your very stylish scented candle, or really want to learn how to play professional ping pong through hiring you as a private tutor — but does your customer NEED it desperately right now?

Think about this book. Why did I choose to write this book now instead of continuing to build my photography business? Because people NEED this now. Our entire economy has shifted. The demand has changed. Think about where people are willing to spend their money now. Think about how you can actually provide a product that helps them.

To close out this lesson, let's score a couple ideas:

Idea: Subscription box for survival essentials including food supplies, toilet paper, and sanitizer sprays.

Passion: 5
Income Potential: 7
Ease: 3
Current Demand: 6
Total Score: 21

If this idea had launched at the outset of the pandemic, it would have been in very high demand. After the supply chain was able to get back on track, the demand for survival goods and toilet paper is back to normal. That being said, it would have been very difficult to secure many of the in demand items like toilet paper and hand sanitizer during the initial phase of the pandemic.

If the idea of a subscription box sounds exciting, there are sites like CrateJoy that make box fulfilment very easy if you still want to give this idea a go. There can be solid income potential with a subscription box as long as you are skilled at protecting your margin, finding interesting items and working the shipping into your prices.

Idea: Local junk removal service.

Passion: 5
Income Potential: 7
Ease: 5
Current Demand: 6
Total Score: 23

Junk removal isn't going anywhere, especially in urban areas where consumption is high. If you look at the success of 1-800-GOTJUNK, it's clear that even an idea as 'unsexy' as junk removal can be scaled to a real, thriving business. If you're passionate about eco friendly ways to manage waste or recycling and love manual labor, this might be a great match!

SUMMARY OF THIS LESSON'S ACTION ITEMS:

- Score each of your ideas according to the chart in the lesson. Be objective here and don't spend too much time over analyzing each score. Even a rough estimate will still give you strong clues into the success potential of each idea.
- If none of your ideas feel like they score high enough for you to feel excited about bringing them to the next lessons, go back and repeat the brainstorming lesson with a fresh start.

TIP:

If you reach this point and don't feel any of your ideas are scoring high enough, it might also be a good idea to get a second opinion from some friends. You can have them read this chapter and tell them about your ideas. Then have them score it based on your explanations. You'd be surprised at how things can be different based on an outside perspective.

LESSON 8:
VISUALIZE YOUR
IDEAS AT SCALE

LESSON 8 DETAILS

So, you now have some ideas for your business, and you've scored them on four qualities to understand their potential. Now, it's time to think about the future. You obviously want to grow your business once you get things moving, so you need to think about what that might look like. In Lesson 9, we'll explore how you feel about your ideas intrinsically and how they align with your values and motivations, but for now, we need to be more pragmatic.

This means thinking about how your ideas will scale. While we've mentioned scale in previous lessons, it's time to really get a grip on how to create a business that can build leverage for the long haul.

You can use the handy table at the end of this chapter to visualize how your business could move in both a linear fashion and how it might grow exponentially. But first, let's establish what scaling means and the different types of scale available.

What is scalability?

Scalability is a measure of how well a business can grow without putting strain on its existing resources. Put simply, it measures your business' ability to make more money over time, without falling apart at the seams. While you might be able to hire more people for your business, if this costs more than the amount of extra money you can make with these additional workers, you're not scaling your business.

However, if you can train your existing workforce to do things faster, making you more money within a shorter time frame at no extra cost, you've just scaled your business! So, while scaling often means making things larger – i.e., making your business larger with more staff, equipment or property – it can simply be a case of making your business more efficient.

So there's basically two types of scale: linear and exponential. I learned about this concept from Eric Siu.

A linear relationship means one variable has a directly proportional effect on another variable. An example of this would be hiring more staff to increase revenue. If your profits increase by roughly the same amount with each additional employee, your business is scaling linearly. Likewise, if you add a new coaching client, and see your profits increase by a similar or predictable amount each time you add a new client, this is linear scaling.

Exponential scalability involves compounding growth: the effort and energy you put into one variable creates an exponential increase in growth over time. If our coaching business owner decides to take her 10 best coaching sessions and turn them into a book, she's now able to sell those 10 hours to a virtually unlimited number of clients. The effort has been shifted from trading one-on-one time with her clients (linear) to creating something that can be purchased by many clients around the world at the same time (exponential).

Let's go over a few different examples:

- A restaurant chain might be linearly scaled if growth means opening new locations around town that each bring in similar revenue with similar overhead costs.

- The same restaurant chain might be exponentially scaling if they start selling cooking lessons online and distributing their most popular sauces in retail stores like Whole Foods.
- A photographer would be linearly scaling when she takes on more photoshoots and hires a team to handle the shoots she can't be at.
- The same photographer can scale exponentially by listing her photographs for sale on stock photo websites and print on demand sites, creating NFT's from her work, or teaching her techniques in an online course.

You don't need to start with the scaled version at the beginning. Instead, you just need to understand whether or not your business has the potential to be scaled, and how you can use your cash flow from your early business to set the stage for exponential growth.

You don't want to get stuck in a non-scaleable idea. This usually involves doing the same things over and over again, without seeing any real growth. Nobody will ask you to scale, so it's on you to make things happen. You can join my online community for more tips on how to break through the next level on your scaling journey. There are also some foundational suggestions in the later lessons of the book that can point you in the right direction.

Because I know you want more examples, here are some different business models that illustrate what linear and exponential scaling looks like in the wild:

EXAMPLE 1 – ILLUSTRATOR

An illustrator's progression in scaling might look like this:

- Non-scaled version: Freelancing by selling services on Fiverr
- Linear scaling: Managing a team of illustrators and growing a studio
- Exponential scaling: Creating a children's book series and selling worldwide on Amazon and other book sites

EXAMPLE 2 – FITNESS COACH

A fitness coach might approach scaling like this:

- Non-scaled version: One-on-one coaching sessions
- Linear scaling 1: Group sessions (virtual and in-person)
- Linear scaling 2: Managing a gym or a team of coaches
- Exponential scaling 1: Selling training manuals or digital workouts
- Exponential scaling 2: Creating a line of fitness apparel

EXAMPLE 3 – DROP SHIPPER

A drop shipper progression in scaling might look like this:

- Non-scaled version: Managing a shop and marketing a few products
- Linear scaling: More shops or managing a team of drop shippers all with their own shops
- Exponential scaling: Create your own product and set up fulfillment with your factory connections

Alright, now it's time to take your ideas and drop them in the future scale projection table below. The 'effort needed' column can be an estimate to help you quantify how hard each path will be, it doesn't need to be exact. Scale the effort on a 1-10 scale where one is easy and 10 is insane.

Business Idea	Linearly Scaled Version	Effort Needed	Exponentially Scaled Version	Effort Needed

SUMMARY OF THIS LESSON'S ACTION ITEMS:

- Take some time to think about what the exponentially scaled version of each of your ideas might look like. Think about the effort you'll need to put in to take your idea from the non-scaled version to the fully scaled version.
- For the purpose of this lesson, the assignment is to simply write each progression of your ideas in the table below and make a note of how hard each stage of scalability is likely to be. You won't be asked to build the exponentially scaled version of your idea at the beginning, but it will be helpful when making your final decision for which business idea to choose.

TIP:

Chances are, as you start to visualize the different paths ahead, you will come up with a lot of new ideas. Many of which may or may not be feasible right now, but that doesn't mean you have to trash them completely. You can create a place to store all the ideas that might be good for a day in the future when you're ready. I learned about a thing called a 'Maybe Someday' folder from David Allen's *Getting Things Done* book and have been implementing it ever since.

Personally, I use a list in the Reminders app on my Macbook and iPhone to store all the ideas that I get from sudden inspiration, but don't want to execute on currently. Every few months I'll revisit this list and update it.

You can also use another note taking or list building app like Evernote, Notion, Asana, Trello, or even a good journal you keep in a handy place. Your 'Maybe Someday' folder will do wonders to keep those ideas from bouncing around in your head begging for your immediate attention. By jotting them down, you give them a proper acknowledgement and then move on to more pressing matters.

LESSON 9: VISUALIZE YOURSELF LIVING THE IDEA

SURPRISES ARE WONDERFUL FOR BIRTHDAYS OR VACATIONS,

BUT WHEN IT COMES TO BUSINESS...

YOU WANT TO AVOID SURPRISES AT ALL COST.

LESSON 9

ESPECIALLY IF THE 'SURPRISE' IS THAT YOUR BUSINESS IDEA TURNS OUT TO BE A DEAD END.

BOOM!!

THE GOOD NEWS IS YOU DON'T HAVE TO BE A VISIONARY TO IMAGINE THE FUTURE.

IF YOU FOLLOW THE SIMPLE STEPS IN THIS CHAPTER, YOU'LL HAVE A MORE CLEAR VISION OF YOUR COMPANY'S FUTURE

AND BE BETTER PREPARED FOR ANY SURPRISES THAT POP UP ALONG THE WAY

LESSON 9 DETAILS

The sad reality we must accept is that some passions are fleeting. If you don't have a deep burning desire to see a project through even the boring times, then you're likely to give up as soon as you hit a roadblock.

It's important to align your project or idea with a long term motivation that can persevere through whatever boring or challenging times await you. This lesson will give you a framework to discover long term motivations for your business idea and save yourself the burnout of choosing an idea you will grow to dread later.

The way that I've found to determine if an idea is something I'll be excited about months down the road is through listing the long term motivations associated with each business idea, and then weighing them against the profit timeline.

Some business ideas can bring you wonderful networking opportunities that are worth more than the monetary value. Other businesses might help you to discover new skills and grow as a person. If learning to lead a team is important to you, it might make it easier to push a promising business to the level where you can hire great people.

The reason I chose to write this book, even though it wouldn't pay off for a long time, was because I knew that the book would be able to serve my long term motivation of creating more content, helping others build businesses, and also give me a product I can sell to many people at once. The skills and experience I would gain were also more than enough motivation to keep going when I got bored or frustrated along the way. And as you can see, the book is now complete!

If your primary motivation is money, you're going to have a tough time staying motivated if profits ever dip. In business, one of the greatest skills you'll need is perseverance. You'll need the burning desire to push through even when you don't feel like working. You'll need the tenacity to doggedly keep at problems until you can find a solution. Sadly, if money is the only motivation, it's not very likely to keep you motivated enough in the long run.

The point of this lesson is to attempt to look into the future and predict all the things that might happen with your business and your motivation. As you venture out on this idea, will you be motivated enough to see it through? Do you have enough long term motivators tied to the idea to balance out the hard work that will be required? Will there be enough monetary rewards down the road?

Once we identify the long term motivations behind each idea, your next step is to imagine yourself going through with the business in as much detail as possible. Let each idea be a totally real possibility.

Not sure how to put this in action? Try this:

- Incubate the ideas in your mind for a day or two.
- Start talking about them to your friends and family.

- Maybe even go so far as to interview someone who would be your potential customer.

Ultimately, your goal during this phase is to visualize yourself going down this path. What would it look like? How would you deal with the boring times, the good times? Who would you partner with? How would you get customers?

Will it make money right away, or will there be a waiting period? Think about all the minute details: ordering supplies, building a website, helping a customer. Try to visualize the whole experience, good and bad.

Once you let yourself go on this imaginary adventure through this new business, how did you feel? Was it as exciting as you thought it would be? Did it suck?

The important thing is, don't feel obligated to make your decision in this lesson. We're giving each idea a viable chance to make it to the final round of our decision making process during the next lesson.

SUMMARY OF THIS LESSON'S ACTION ITEMS:

- Write down three to five long term motivations that are tied to each business idea. These can be "shallow" motivations like fame or notoriety, meeting attractive people, or making lots of money. They can also be tied to personal growth or skill development. They can also be related to a cause you care deeply about.
- Visualize your future self embarking on the journey of seeing this business idea through. Imagine yourself working hard on this business in detail. Talk to your friends about how it works, talk to competitors and people who might be a customer to understand how the real day-to-day goes down.

LESSON 10: PICK A WINNER

LESSON 10 DETAILS

Alright, here's the moment of truth. Go ahead and choose one of your ideas to run with.

You don't have to do this idea forever, but it's important to choose one and start moving forward. You'll have to be okay with putting the other ideas on the backburner until the time is right. You need to devote 100% of your available energy to his new idea until one of two things happens:

1. You become profitable and can now scale it.
2. You realize (with certainty) that the idea doesn't make sense financially and you happily check the idea off your bucket list as something you tried, explored, and are finished with.

I'm sure you've heard the saying that ideas are a dime a dozen, and hard work is all that really matters. Unfortunately, that's only partially true: not all ideas are created equal. Some ideas will never be profitable no matter how hard you work at them. We also don't need to worry about finding the perfect idea that will be super profitable instantly, because for most ideas, a little hard work over time can make all the difference in bridging the gap to a thriving, profitable business.

It's okay to kill an idea if it doesn't work out. In fact, what we're trying to do with this step is to reduce the chances of you having to give up on an idea after investing a month of time and energy. The sooner we can eliminate an unviable idea, the better.

That being said, we don't want you to be paralyzed thinking about which idea to choose. Sometimes, the best idea is one that will only appear when starting down the path of another less desirable idea. Indecision is the ultimate dream killer at this stage. Almost more important than earning a profit in this first month is building a habit of momentum and a process for rapid deployment of effort.

So, take a nice deep breath, look at the two or three ideas, and choose your winner.

The other ideas should be stored in a "Maybe Someday" folder in your Notion, Evernote, or personal organization system.

Now, if you just don't feel good about ANY of the ideas you have, you can try two things:

1. Pick the most viable option, even if it's not perfect, and treat it like a JOB until you get to a level where you can start your next idea.
2. Schedule a call with me or a trusted mentor to find an angle that you might have missed on your own. You can book a call with me on my website at www.startbrigade.com.

Whatever you do, *do not pass this point if you haven't picked a single idea*. Remember, there will be time for your other ideas later. If one idea is "just a hobby," that's fine, but treat it as such. You will need to have a very clear order of priority because you will be faced with moments where you will have to choose between one or the other. Make that decision now so you don't have to stress out about it for the next several weeks.

SUMMARY OF THIS LESSON'S ACTION ITEMS:

- Trust in the work that you've put in evaluating your ideas and decide on the ONE idea that you will choose as your side hustle.
- If you don't feel pumped about any of your ideas, consult with a mentor to brainstorm additional options. Of course if you don't have a mentor yet, you can schedule a session with me and together we can zero in on an idea that feels right for you.

LESSON 11:
CREATE YOUR RAPID
FIRE BUSINESS PLAN

DEAD END

IN THIS LESSON, YOUR MISSION IS TO CREATE A BASIC NAVIGATION MAP FOR YOUR BUSINESS.

IT WOULD ALSO SEEM EQUALLY RIDICULOUS TO START DRIVING WITHOUT KNOWING THE GENERAL ROUTE AND DIRECTIONS TO TAKE.

SIMPLY USE THE OUTLINE IN THE NEXT PAGES TO DRAW A BIRDS-EYE VIEW OF HOW YOUR BUSINESS WILL GET STARTED AND START GENERATING SALES.

RATHER THAN GETTING BOGGED DOWN IN THE DETAILS OF EVERY TWIST AND TURN,

LESSON 11 DETAILS

If you're a natural planner and strategizer, you'll love this lesson. If you tend to swing from the hip and favor spontaneity, you'll need this lesson more than anyone, even if you might be itching to skip past the whole planning stage and start building.

Planning is an art on its own. Top project managers earn big bucks making official launch plans for new startups and campaigns. This lesson will distill the process of creating a business plan to a simple 60 minute approach that you can use to guide your efforts to success.

Rather than spend months deliberating between all the possible options for your launch, or rushing in without a plan, we'll use the framework in this lesson to create a simple, effective roadmap to start your business. I call it the Rapid Fire Business Plan

Your mission is to make a basic outline of what you will need to do to launch your business. Later, you can go back and fill this out in more detail. The important thing is to have a loose outline at this stage that only takes you about one hour. The reason we keep this to 60 minutes is so you don't get lost in speculation. We want you out taking action. This plan will serve as a loose blueprint so you're not spinning your wheels. Remember, this is a rough outline, not a Tolstoy novel. Keep it simple.

Set the timer for 10 minutes and start going on your first section. The idea here is to force yourself to build a loose roadmap and think like a project manager. Use short, precise language, like "I sell X to Y," for example "My business helps busy moms find reliable part time nannies."

Instructions: Spend 10 minutes in each of the sections listed below.

1. *Overview:* Describe what the business is and a bird's eye view of how it works.
2. *Customers:* Describe who your customers are and where they hang out.
3. *Revenue Model:* Describe how you get paid, break down the costs for your time and resources. Come up with ballpark pricing.
4. *Competition:* Who is your competition? What is your point of differentiation? What is your competition doing well that you can emulate?
5. *Marketing and Sales:* How will you get customers? This is the most important section and one that a lot of businesses skip over by saying "I'll just run paid advertising" or "I'll just get referrals from friends and family."
6. *Milestones and Next Steps:* What are the clear actionable steps that you'll need to take to get to the next milestones?

   To make this extra simple, your next steps can be these:

   › Create an offer
   › Create a brand (this can be you or a company name)

- ➤ Set up business foundations
  - ▷ Website
  - ▷ Seller's permits
  - ▷ Ordering Supplies/Equipment/Tools
  - ▷ Contacting referral partners
  - ▷ Getting testimonials
- ➤ Set Your Prices
- ➤ Set up payment
- ➤ Get peer feedback on your offer + funnel
- ➤ Launch your offer
- ➤ Promote your offer
- ➤ Get help to spread the word

Show your business plan to someone you respect and who can give you some pointers. Often a fresh set of eyes can save you months of doing something the hard way. Do not let fear of judgement keep you from asking for advice. Sure, you'll figure it out on your own eventually, but it could save you a month or more of experimenting. Wouldn't it be worth asking someone who's done it before?

Additionally, if you have the resources, you can invest in hiring a consultant to look your plan over and share wisdom and recommendations specific to your industry.

You can download the free business plan worksheet on the resources section of my website at www.startbrigade.com.

Note: sometimes your friends and peers will have bad advice. They all mean well, but ultimately, you're the one calling the shots here. You don't need to listen to all the feedback. If it slows you down and keeps you from standing up to the plate and taking a swing, then you just go on and plow forward.

SUMMARY OF THIS LESSON'S ACTION ITEMS:

- Borrow the outline from this lesson and create your 60 minute business plan. You can set a timer for 10 minutes to fill out each of the six sections.
- If you have the resources, contact a mentor or advisor and chat through the business plan to get their input. As many of you might be starting out and haven't found your mentor yet, you can always schedule a strategy session with me to chat through your plan at www.startbrigade.com.

TIP:

You're more than likely going to need a separate business checking account in the coming chapters to make your life (and your accounting) easier. I recommend taking the time to set up a separate checking account for your business at this stage if you don't have one yet. Although checking accounts are fairly easy to set up, you'll have several days that you'll need to process everything and get your account set up. Better to have this done and ready before you'll need it in Lesson 18 and beyond.

My favorite checking account is the Charles Schwab investor checking account. It's free to set up, and this is one of the only checking accounts out there that pays you interest on your balance. You can also use any ATMs worldwide and get all the service fees reimbursed. Overall, it's a very solid checking account to set up for the early stages of your business. You do need to sign up for an investment account to avoid the fees, but you don't actually have to use the investment options.

Keep in mind, you don't necessarily need to have a 'business' account right out of the gate. You can simply opt to have a separate personal checking account until you file your appropriate business entity paperwork. Just be sure to find an account that doesn't charge you fees.

PART 3

BUILD YOUR OFFER

In the coming lessons, you will create an attractive description of your product or service you can use to encourage customers to purchase your stuff. This is called an offer. An offer consists of all the details around your product or service including the pricing, the features or benefits, and of course, the messaging and presentation.

A great offer doesn't just describe what your customer will get when they purchase your product, it also conveys a deeper story that the customer can relate to on an emotional level.

The five lessons and activities in this section will help you accomplish the following:

1. Research what similar products are using to guide potential buyers into paying customers.
2. Research your customers and understand their needs and psychology. You'll ask questions like, "Why do they want my service?" and, "How will their lives be enriched through my product?"
3. Understand what it is about your product that makes it special by honing in on your unique story and highlighting your point of differentiation.
4. You'll also make your product's benefits and features clearly articulated then package these features with powerful and attractive messaging.
5. Finally, you will formulate your research and findings into a clear and compelling offer.

LESSON 12:
HUNT IN THE WILD
FOR INSPIRATION

THE GOOD NEWS IS THESE CLUES ARE ALL LEFT BY THE BUSINESSES WHO CAME DOWN THIS PATH BEFORE YOU!

WHEN YOU'RE NOT SURE HOW TO STRUCTURE YOUR ADVERTISING CAMPAIGN, GO STUDY YOUR COMPETITORS

IT'S HIGHLY LIKELY THAT THEY'VE INVESTED COUNTLESS HOURS TESTING THE DIFFERENT PATHS TO ATTRACT CUSTOMERS.

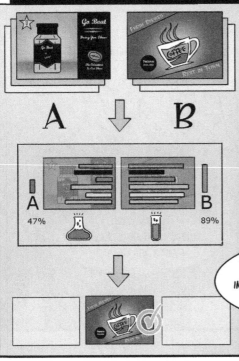

SO, IN THIS LESSON, YOUR MISSION IS TO INFILTRATE YOUR COMPETITION'S SALES PROCESS FROM A-Z.

I'LL GIVE YOU SOME TOOLS TO DO THIS IN THE LESSON DETAILS.

LESSON 12 DETAILS

TIMELINE: DAY 12
ESTIMATED TIME TO COMPLETE: 40 MIN.

In this lesson, you get to play detective, spy, or an amazing researcher. If I were to call this "competitive analysis," your eyes would probably glaze over and you'd put this guide down and go back to fantasizing about one day finally having your own business instead of actually doing it. So I won't call it that. I'll call it *hunting in the wild* instead.

The reason this step is so powerful is that a lot of what you're trying to do has already been done a million times in some form or fashion. There is absolutely no reason for you to go and reinvent the wheel. The sooner we can build you an effective offer, the sooner you'll be able to enjoy your new life of entrepreneurial success.

And so, it all starts with looking at what your competition has produced in the past and is currently using or testing. If your competition is selling to a similar audience, even better. You'll be able to learn from their efforts and save time implementing your own offers.

Now, I should put a disclaimer here: it's not okay to steal. You can use what others are doing as a guide, as inspiration, even as a template, but the final result should be of your own construction.

You'll want to compile a folder or document that neatly organizes your inspiration from your competition as well as additional resources and guides. You can call this a swipe file, a white sheet, an inspiration board, or one of my personal favorites: a Hunting Trail (That's from Todd Henry).

We'll use the term *swipe file* moving forward to define any collection of resources, research or inspiration from others that you can apply to your own projects. You can have swipe files for a number of things:

1. Advertisements (digital or print)
2. Images (websites, ads, or social posts)
3. Copywriting/Messaging (that means sales language — typically used in advertisements, checkout pages or general website marketing)

There are lots of great resources for building your custom swipe files:

1. **Pinterest:** Type in your keywords and boom! You'll be presented with tons of visuals from other creators. Pay attention to promoted posts. You can click on those posts and swipe their sales pages to start building your own sales page swipe file.
2. **Facebook Ad Library:** It's a free database of the ads being run on Facebook. It's one of the most powerful tools to see what ads your competition is running. (Note: this doesn't show all the ads out there, especially if your competition is spending smaller amounts.)

3. **Your Competition's Facebook Pages:** You can literally get a chronological timeline of all the marketing efforts your competition has tried by going to their Facebook page. Look at their previous ads and promotions to see an idea for what worked for them. You can also pay attention to the engagement and comments. If a particular post got a ton of engagement, there's a reason why. You can also look for the posts that your competition has been publishing consistently. If they keep posting the same image for a long time, that image is obviously still working for them.

4. **LandingFolio.com:** This is a beautiful site to get inspiration for other websites. You can browse landing pages, pricing pages, and even snag templates for your own site. You can filter by industry and color scheme.

5. **Increase.Academy:** This is a copywriting website by Sean Vossler that has tons of training available to go through. Some of their training is premium, but they have plenty of free options available as well.

6. **Swiped.co, blogs like honeycopy.com, and Neville Medhora's Kopywriting Kourse:** These are a few great places to go for free and premium resources on copywriting. (There are a ton of these blogs and resources out there, find a few you can add to your swiped file, and keep hunting when inspiration runs dry.)

7. **Craigslist:** Remember this? Craigslist is still a gold mine to find examples of people writing offers and pitching services. If you can sift through the bad grammar and spam, you might just find an offer you like in there.

Once you've accumulated enough inspiration to have a good idea of how your competition is promoting to their customers, you're ready to start thinking how your customers would actually respond to each type of advertisement and offer. That means understand who your customer is and what they are looking for.

As you do your research in the wild, scanning your competition and other sites, it will become important to organize your findings by stages in the marketing journey. Your swipe file can be organized in the same manner. Keep all the advertisements that speak to a customer's first impression of a product in one place. Perhaps these are Facebook ads, or social media posts, or sponsored blog articles on popular sites — whatever material would be presented to a stranger.

The next category might be the stuff a company will present to people who are looking at the product. This might be a list of features and benefits, or a video showcasing how the service works. Then there might be a section where you find inspiration around the selling process: what do your competitors present to potential customers as they are in the checkout process, either on a sales call or on a purchase page. (You might have to get on the phone and actually experience what your competition does here.)

Finally, what does the followup process look like? How do your competitors deliver the experience after presenting a sales pitch, or visiting the sales page? What do they present buyers on the thank you page after purchasing?

The more *spy work* you can pull off here, the less *guess* work you will have to do as you build your own offer.

SUMMARY OF THIS LESSON'S ACTION ITEMS:

- Identify three or four competitors who you will use for inspiration.
- Create a swipe file of your competitors ads, social posts, website work flows, and overall experience.
- Spend at least 20 minutes to go through your competitors sales processes and collect the research you find in your swipe file. The more specific and detailed you are, the more clear your own path will become.

TIP:

You're more than likely going to need a separate business check- When it comes to creating a swipe file the keys to success are consistency and ease of access.

Whatever tool you set up should be easy for you to use on the fly, as you're browsing media. You should also always use the same process for adding things to your swipe file so things don't get jumbled.

My favorite tools for creating swipe files are Pinterest, Notion or Google Docs. You can bookmark whatever list you are using in your browser so that any time you see something cool you know where to drop it.

Pinterest makes things easy with boards that have distinct urls. Notion has similar features, but also allows for other types of files and text entries.

LESSON 13:
GET IN YOUR
CUSTOMERS SHOES

LESSON 13 DETAILS

One of the most important rules in marketing is that customer development is never finished. It's an ongoing process to further empathize with the people who are buying from you, ask for their feedback, and implement their needs into your product and product messaging.

Now I get it, you don't actually have any customers yet — that's fine. At the beginning, we're going to rely on your intuition. We're assuming that you've chosen your idea because you have at least enough passion to carry it through. Based on that assumption, you probably already have a deep understanding of your future customers and their pain points. Now, our mission in this section is to get that into writing.

We are hoping to understand the customer as much as possible, so that when we write the offer, it will feel like we really understand their needs, making it easy for them to jump in and make a purchase.

Write out a description of your customer and keep this handy for future reference. You'll want to include some of these basics:

Who are your customers:

1. Age/Gender
2. Education Level
3. Income Level
4. Passions and Interests
5. Pain Points

Where are they hanging out:

1. Social platforms
2. Deal sites
3. Competition sites
4. Blogs and Podcasts

The development of your customer is never done. At the beginning, you might only have a theoretical customer, so it's okay to gather this information through guessing and researching forums where your customers are hanging out.

As you begin to gain momentum with your business, it's critical that you take the time to engage with your customers and ask them serious questions about their experiences with your product. Think outside of the box and ask them questions that can provide deep insights. "Did you like the product?" is not as powerful of a question as, "If you had a magic wand and could change anything about the product, what would it be able to do for you?" You want to survey your customers and start conversations that go beyond yes/no answers.

You can then use these responses as a guiding star to point you in the right direction of making a better product and, just as importantly, a better offer.

SUMMARY OF THIS LESSON'S ACTION ITEMS:

- Spend some time doing deep research into who your customers are and what they are passionate about. Take scrupulous notes that encompass all the factors, like age, demographics, and interests. From there, you will take this research and bring it to the next action step.
- Write a buyer's persona and make it as detailed as possible so you can understand what your customers are going through and their psychological motivations for wanting your product. You can use the buyer persona worksheet available in the resources section of my website at www. startbrigade.com.

TIP:

If you want a tool that you can use to gather some really powerful responses from your customers, you can use a survey. Three options for great survey tools I recommend are Typeform, SurveyMonkey, and of course, Google Forms. All of these are super easy to set up and collect responses in one central place.

If you are already using Airtable for database management, you can also set up surveys in there for collecting customer feedback, but the level of complexity might be beyond your needs at the beginning.

If you haven't been able to get customers yet, you can still send a survey to people who are like your future customers by finding them in a Facebook group. If you ask nicely and make sure your survey only takes a few minutes to complete, most people will be happy to help.

LESSON 14: ELEMENTS OF A GREAT OFFER AND YOUR POINT OF DIFFERENTIATION

LESSON 14 DETAILS

Why do we buy from one brand and not another? What is it about a particular product that makes us open our wallet and make a purchase? Apart from being positioned in the right place at the right time, much of this decision making process is dependent on the story the product conveys to us.

A really good offer will have this story baked into it in a way that draws the customer in, shows them how the product can solve their needs, and then spins the story of the product in a way that makes it more desirable than other solutions.

So how do you create a story around your product that your customers will resonate with?

It all starts with empathy. You'll need to understand what your customers are going through, and align your messaging and your offer's presentation to speak to that thing your customers are experiencing. Empathy is more than psychological tricks or flashy sales language, it's caring about the well being of the other person.

Yes, you're in this to make money, but if you're not also contributing a worthwhile experience to the customer then you're going to have a hard time making money long-term. Sure, people do it, but ultimately they're labeled as scammers or slimeballs. There's a lot of reasons why great companies are successful, but if you look closely, empathy seems to be a huge differentiating factor between cult success and market flop.

Take GoPro for example. GoPro was able to achieve such incredible success attributed it to, you guessed it, empathy. GoPro was founded by people who were adventurous and wanted to make videos while out on the waves or in the wild. They understood the needs and culture of this tribe that would be out on the go. Another camera company like Panasonic or Sony could have certainly come up with the idea for GoPro and brought it to market, but without the empathy to understand what this type of consumer was going through, they would be hard pressed to build the cult following GoPro has achieved.

The marketing or product development team at Panasonic was probably not rappelling down cliffs or chasing 20 foot waves out on a remote island. However, even if you're not directly involved in the experience of your consumer, you can use empathy to understand their needs and what they're going through.

In the last lesson, we went deep into your target customer's mindset and background. In this lesson, we're going to work to tie your offer to those needs by creating a story they will resonate with.

Your Point of Differentiation and How to Find It

The goal is to find a point of differentiation in your product or your story that makes you and your mission relevant to a customer on an emotional level. Think about what you stand for, and why you're pursuing this path. We'll then work on the messaging to make this cause of yours shine in the offer.

Before we start writing this down in an offer, let's think about some different ways we can incorporate a point of differentiation into your messaging that will resonate with your customers.

Method One: Champion a cause

You can do this by championing a cause you care about. An example of this in action might be the early days of Los Angeles based apparel manufacturing company American Apparel. Their famous approach to create high quality garments being a local manufacturer was an ideological stance that set them apart from their competitors.

When a customer was making a choice between a t-shirt manufactured somewhere in another country in unknown working conditions, or a t-shirt that was promised to be produced in Los Angeles, customers who valued locally produced products would choose American Apparel because the story of the brand connected to their values.

American Apparel also clearly highlighted this point of differentiation in every advertisement they made. "Made in USA, Sweatshop Free" became more than just a fact, it became a culture. If you have a cause you're championing with your brand, put that front and center in your offer with a clear, one or two sentence statement that people can contextualize at a glance.

Method Two: Be the paradigm shift

You can also have your point of differentiation be a stylistic preference or a change in industry standards. Are the majority of competitors in your space missing a sense of design or aesthetic that can be the edge in your products? Do your competitors tend to be unsympathetic and provide poor customer service? You'll want to look for that thing that can give you an unfair advantage (cheat code), and stand out from the crowd.

During the 80's, while IBM was focused on creating no-nonsense business computers, Apple highlighted the fact that it was preferred by forward thinking creative types. Your point of differentiation can be as concrete as a type of material used, or as intangible as an ideology. Whatever that point of differentiation is, let that be the banner your customers can rally behind. In your offer, state it clearly and succinctly so that people can remember it.

Method Three: Have an origin story

Your point of differentiation can also be your origin story. Often, the motivation behind why you decide to begin your new side hustle will have a lot of emotional power that your audience can latch on to as they read your offer. If you can distill the reasons you embarked on this journey into a compelling origin story that explains why you're going against all the odds, taking a risk, and putting yourself out there, you'll have one undeniable point of differentiation.

For an example of a brand that used the origin story as a means to establish their point of differentiation, let's take a look at Jessica Alba and the Honest Co. The origin story of the Honest Co. was about how as a new mother, Alba was looking for non-toxic and safe cleaning products to use, but couldn't find them. So the Honest Co. was supposed to bring non-deceptive and natural household products to the market so people could trust what they were using to clean with.

Interestingly enough, with a point of differentiation like that, Alba's company faced a number of lawsuits for not being as forthright with the ingredients as promised in the company's creed. Regardless, the origin story can be a powerful way to get people to buy in with your mission and become attached to your product on an emotional level.

SUMMARY OF THIS LESSON'S ACTION ITEMS:

- Summarize who your offer is written for. Get as detailed as possible. You want it to feel like you belong to a tribe, a family, or a close knit community.
- Think about what your point of differentiation is and write it out in a clear, simple phrase or combination of phrases. You should be able to get this point across to a total stranger in a 5 to 10 second conversation. Your point of differentiation could be an origin story, a stylistic choice, or a meaningful ideological cause.

LESSON 15: HOW TO PACKAGE YOUR OFFER WITH THE RIGHT MESSAGING

EVEN IF YOUR PRODUCT IS DIFFERENT, SPECIAL, OR UNIQUE, NO ONE WILL BUY IT IF THEY DON'T UNDERSTAND WHAT IT DOES.

TO CONVEY THIS, YOU WILL NEED TO PACKAGE YOUR PRODUCT IN A WAY THAT'S SUPER RELEVANT TO YOUR CUSTOMERS.

YOU CAN FIND THIS RELEVANCE THROUGH LISTING OUT ALL THE FEATURES AND BENEFITS YOUR CUSTOMERS WILL EXPERIENCE WHEN BUYING YOUR OFFERING.

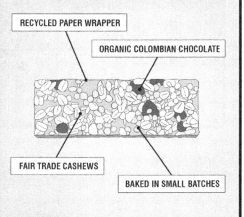

THE FEATURES OF YOUR PRODUCT ARE THINGS LIKE THE MATERIALS USED, THE FREQUENCY OF SERVICE SESSIONS, OR THE LEVEL OF DETAIL PROVIDED.

RECYCLED PAPER WRAPPER

ORGANIC COLOMBIAN CHOCOLATE

FAIR TRADE CASHEWS

BAKED IN SMALL BATCHES

LESSON 15 DETAILS

A great offer has more than just a story about how it's different than the rest out there. A great offer should also describe what your product or service does. These are often called the features of the product or the service. Your features should be simple, clear and easy to understand. For the purpose of this lesson, take a pen and paper out and start writing a list of all the things your product or service does. You could also write about some of the materials it's made of if it's a physical product.

Once your list has about 20 to 30 features, it's time to start thinking about the benefits that your customer will experience when they purchase your product or service. A great offer will paint a picture of how the customer's life will be impacted through the experience of purchasing it. Those impact points are called benefits. Where a feature might be something like 'fast delivery' the benefit might be along the lines of 'so that you can save time' or 'so that you don't have to leave your house'.

In order to uncover some very potent benefits and not just the surface level stuff, grab your pen and paper and write down another list of 20 to 30 benefits. To make this easy, try using the phrase "Purchase X **so that** you can Y" where 'X' is your product and 'Y' is the benefit your customer will have after purchasing your product.

The final element we'll need is a call to action, or CTA. This is basically the instruction that you will give your customer for how to take advantage of your offer. You can use something like a free strategy call if you plan on continuing to pitch them on the phone or on a webinar, or you can state the price and have a link to make a purchase. You might even encourage them to visit your upcoming event and to RSVP on a link. Eventually you will experiment and find the CTA that gives you the best results.

Your full offer will include these elements:

- Your point of differentiation clearly stated
- Nice, simple description of the most important features
- A clear description of who the product is for
- A powerful statement of the benefits the customer can experience
- A simple CTA that gives them something to do after reading the offer

Here's an example of an offer that incorporates a little of all of the above:

After years of suffering from obesity and leaky gut, I created the perfect Paleo meal plan for busy moms. It's full of easy, 30 minute recipes so that you can feel good about what you eat and still have time to help the kids finish homework. Download now for only $19.

In this example, there's an origin story and a point of differentiation in one. The origin story says how the creator was suffering for years trying to find a solution and finally had to create it herself. The offer is also very specific about whom it's for: busy moms. It also makes it easy to understand what the features of the product are: Paleo meal plans with easy, 30 minute recipes. It then paints a picture of the benefits of eating healthy beyond solving the obesity and leaky gut issues by emphasizing the time saved and the real benefit of being able to spend more time with the kids. Finally, the offer has a price and instructions for how to purchase the meal plan.

Sometimes, you can use images or video to tell some of these stories, but for the sake of our first offer, let's aim to simply get all the individual components listed out first. In the next lessons, you'll put everything together and even build a sales page.

SUMMARY OF THIS LESSON'S ACTION ITEMS:

- Write out 20 to 30 of the many things your product does, and how it does them. Think about ways to minimize complexity and describe the features as simple as possible. List as many features of your service as you can, in a way that people can understand at a glance.
- Write out 20 to 30 benefits of your product. You can write it using the "so that you can ____" prompt if it helps you gather ideas faster.
- Write a CTA that either includes a price and instructions to purchase, or has the instructions for continuing to the next stage of your sales pipeline. Examples: RSVP, learn more, get a strategy call, watch the webinar, etc.

LESSON 16:
JUST WRITE THE THING

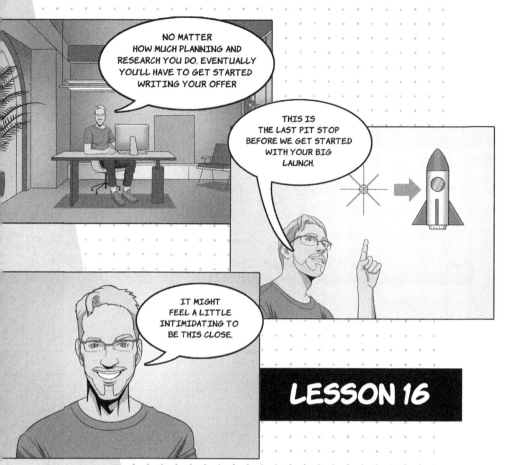

LESSON 16

LESSON 16 DETAILS

TIMELINE: DAY 16
ESTIMATED TIME TO COMPLETE: 30 MIN.

If you study any copywriting course out there, one of the common themes you'll encounter is the amount of offers you'll need to write in order to get a winning offer.

Let's take a guess. How many offers do you think it takes to "get it right?"

If you said, "A whole lot of them!" you're right! Great copywriters know that their best work doesn't come with the first attempt. Usually, the best ads and offers are hidden beneath layers and layers of mediocre offers. As Eric Siu often says, "You gotta get the 'suck' out before you can be great."

So in this lesson, your mission is to write 12 offers and choose the best one to run with. At this point, you've done your research into who your customers are and what they're looking for. You know their pain points inside and out. You can spew off two dozen powerful reasons why purchasing your product will greatly improve their lives. You've even built a database and swipe file of your competitor's ads and offers. You have insights into how your competition is making the emotional connection to the customer and is making a profit.

With that said, you are fully prepared to create a powerful, functioning offer. There's no reason why it won't work. All you have to do is make the damn thing. It's waiting inside of you. It's ready to spill onto the page.

But because this is a new task, it might feel like a lot of pressure. That's why we're making 12 offers. The first three to four are going to be crap. That's cool. You gotta get them out of the way and get the fears cast out. Once you actually start writing the offers, your subconscious is going to stop grumbling and telling you all the reasons why you shouldn't make the thing. Once you start writing, your subconscious will be forced to play along. You've already given your mind all the tools it needs to do the job, now trust that you'll make something out of it.

Here's what I want you to do in this lesson: I want you to get yourself to a place where you have all your research, inspiration and training set nearby for quick reference. Then, get comfortable at your writing station — clear all the distractions you might have for the next 45 minutes. Go into airplane mode: no phone, no internet browsing, no text messages, no social media. You get the idea.

Have whatever you need to "get in the zone" prepared and set aside. I prefer a hot drink like tea or coffee, noise canceling headphones playing techno or classical music, and a sparkling clean workstation. Then, set a timer for 45 minutes and let the ideas start flowing.

Don't stop until you have at least 12 offers on the page. Remember, the more time you spend on this to get it right, the less work it will be to convince your customer to choose you when you launch your offer, so don't stop at eight. Keep pushing.

Once your offer is running, you'll want to come back and refresh it frequently. You'll get better every time you do this exercise, so keep coming back to it every month or so. At the early stages of a launch, you'll probably want to refresh things twice a month. After you've gotten some traction, you'll probably only need to refresh your offer every three to four months.

After you've written 12 offers, you're bound to have a few that are going to feel right. Let's take those and launch them in the next chapter.

SUMMARY OF THIS LESSON'S ACTION ITEMS:

- Write 12 unique versions of your offer until it starts to feel irresistible.
- Present your offer to a mentor or friend for feedback. There might be some small tweak they suggest that makes a big difference.
- Go ahead and choose the offer you will use to launch in the following lessons. Don't worry, you can always make changes after you start to get feedback from your buyers.

PART 4
LAUNCHING YOUR OFFER

It's time to do this! It's finally time for the big moment of truth, the great launch week, the big kahuna of side hustles. In the next few lessons, we're going to get your business ready to service paying customers.

This section will present a massive shift in the approach to the exercises. Where Parts 1 through 3 have been largely focused on research and planning, Part 4 will pivot to action. You'll be building all the nuts and bolts of your sales system and setting up your launch campaign.

The four lessons in this section will cover the following ideas and action points:

1. Setting up a sales page so you can actually make money from your customers.
2. Running a test sale so you don't have any embarrassing malfunctions when you get a real customer.
3. Performing a soft launch to stress test your offer and make sure everything is ready to go.
4. And finally, the big official launch where you'll unveil your side hustle in all its glory.

LESSON 17: SETTING UP YOUR SALES PAGE

THE OFFER YOU JUST MADE TELLS YOUR CUSTOMERS WHAT THEY'LL BE GETTING WHEN THEY BUY YOUR STUFF.

LESSON 17

NOW YOU NEED A PLACE TO KEEP THEM FROM CHICKENING OUT, AND ACTUALLY GIVING YOU MONEY: YOUR SALES PAGE

A GOOD SALES PAGE IS DESIGNED TO IGNITE A DESIRE TO PURCHASE IN THE CUSTOMERS WHO VISIT THE PAGE.

AN EFFICIENT SALES PAGE IS OPTIMIZED TO REDUCE THE AMOUNT OF VISITORS WHO COME TO THE STORE, BUT DON'T PURCHASE

LESSON 17 DETAILS

Now I know you're excited to get out and show your offer to the public, but if you don't have a system in place to convert all that interest and attention into cash, you'll have wasted a lot of energy.

Imagine seeing a billboard for a delicious cheeseburger restaurant on the next exit of the highway. You're hungry, the cheeseburger looks like a great idea and the price is right. So you decide to exit the freeway and drive to the restaurant parking lot. As you get out of your car and start to walk in, you suddenly realize that the restaurant doesn't exist! It's just an empty plot of land with a big sign. Well, there's not much you can do but scratch your head and drive off looking for a different restaurant.

That's what it's like if you have an offer without a sales page. You need a platform where you can fulfill your customers' orders. When setting up your sales page, you want to predict all the possible things that can get in the way of your customer successfully completing their order. Anything that stands between your customer and a sale should be removed or solved.

The goal of our sales page is to maximize the revenue from the people who are coming to your business from the offer you present. Fundamentally, we have two methods of optimizing the revenue potential of your sales page:

1. Increase the likelihood that customers who visit your shop/site make a purchase, and
2. Increase the average transaction value of each customer.

There are a number of experiments and adjustments you can make to play to adjust those two inputs, but we'll lay the foundation for the initial draft of your sales page in this lesson. You can always go and refine it as you start to collect feedback along the way.

Writing the Sales Page Language:

Let's assume your advertisement or promotion has been effective and your soon to be customer has embarked on their long, perilous journey and arrived on your sales page. The goal here is to keep them from turning tail and smashing that 'close tab' button at all costs.

The good news is that other businesses have spent countless hours testing this very phenomenon and have some really good best practices you can swipe and deploy on your own sales page.

First, you'll need a good headline. Just like your offer, it's important we're connecting your product to the transformation your customer will have after purchasing. When they visit your sales page after seeing your offer, it should feel like the promise you make is attainable at the bottom of your sales page. The purpose of the headline here is to keep them reading more. You've piqued their curiosity, now invoke desire. Use your headline to paint a picture of what life can be like after having your product in their hands.

Not sure what to write in your headline? Go snoop around a few reputable sites in your niche and you should get some clues. Borrow the good stuff and make it your own.

Now, with the rest of the content on your sales page, we want to get the customer to keep reading, but also remind them why they need your product. Illustrate the many problems that they have without your solution.

You can then show that these problems are, in fact, solvable. Show them life can be improved with your solution. Then, reassure them that your product is the best solution by expressing the features and the benefits it provides. Really highlight your point of differentiation here. What makes your product special? Tell a story.

You can also drop in some powerful social proof or testimonials that demonstrate the effectiveness of your product. You want to handle the objections they might have to purchasing here on the sales page.

Some additional resources you can use to enhance your sales process and handle any customer objections along the way might include:

- Reviews or testimonials
- Webinars
- Over the phone sales calls or consultations
- Videos or product demos
- Images or GIFs
- Free or discounted trials/samples that give a taste of your product and encourage the customer to pay for the full package

Finally, let's give them an offer they can't refuse! If you've done your work in the earlier steps, this should be easy. You've written all the reasons why your product will benefit the customer, you've demonstrated that your product is high quality, now all you have to do is present them a fair price and let them make their decision.

If they choose to say no, that's fine. You've done your part in attempting to solve their problem. They'll either say yes to the deal, or go on with their life. You'll get better results as you keep practicing your copywriting skills, but you'll always have to be okay to let a few fish escape the net.

Various types of sales pages:

- The product page of an Amazon item
- The product page of an Etsy or Shopify item
- The Book a Consultation Page of a service business

- The Book a Mini Session Page of a coach
- The Order Page of a subscription box
- The Reserve an Appointment Page of a massage therapist or trainer
- The Gig Description Page of a Fiverr gig
- The Profile Page of a Thumbtack, Bark or TaskRabbit service provider
- The Listing of a Turo Rental Car or AirBnb rental
- The Listing of an Eventbrite, Meetup, or AirBnb Experiences event

Whether you're providing a product or a service, you'll need a sales page to drive your customers automatically to give you money.

Your mission in this section is to complete your sales page. You should do your best to eliminate any friction the buyer might have along the journey and allow them to seamlessly navigate from wanting to purchase to being able to give you their money. That means having a reliable payment collection method directly on your sales page, or in your sales call.

We'll go into payment methods and test payments in the next section. For this section, your goal is to get all the language and creative assets in place. We'll also connect your offer to your promotional channel in later sections. Right now, we're building the net to catch the fish.

SUMMARY OF THIS LESSON'S ACTION ITEMS:

- Write the text copy for your sales page.
- Add additional features like example images, reviews, and options to book a call or schedule an appointment to help your page have a better visitor to sales conversion ratio.

TIP:

When writing your sales page, try using the UPSYD framework. This is coined from Eugene Schwartz, the author of the cult classic book *Breakthrough Advertising* and one of the most influential advertising pioneers.

The UPSYD framework allows you to share information with your customer in a series of sequential steps and increases their likelihood to purchase from you through progressing along the following states: unaware, problem aware, solution aware, your solution aware, and then, assuming you've sufficiently prepared them, you present them with a deal.

Let's break it down.

Your sales page can be made of 5 parts:

- ▷ U – The attention grabber (unaware)
- ▷ P – Stating the problem (problem aware)
- ▷ S – Unveiling a solution (solution aware)
- ▷ Y – Positioning your product as the best solution (your solution aware)
- ▷ D – And finally, presenting them with an irresistible deal (deal)

LESSON 18:
RUN A TEST SALE

LESSON 18 DETAILS

depending on complexity

If you're taking payments directly on a website, there are a number of free apps you can use. Stripe is probably the best option for digital products, software subscriptions, elearning, and any product or service that is purchased online.

If you plan to have in-person transactions where people are paying you directly, Square is the stronger choice. Both Stripe and Square can handle in-person and online payments, but Stripe is stronger online, and Square is stronger in-person.

You can also use PayPal as your payment method if you are already set up with PayPal or you're having issues integrating Stripe on your website. I ran a production company for several years taking payments exclusively on PayPal, and it worked "just fine." I wouldn't recommend PayPal for a long term solution, however. Some things, like ticket sales on Eventbrite, are powered through PayPal, so you may find yourself using PayPal as your main payment solution.

Whatever payment solution you choose, just make sure it's easy to install on your website or storefront. Most website builders come with the payment integrations ready to go. You'll simply need to log in to the application and fill out your bank information.

In order to accept payments through Stripe or Square, you'll need to set up a bank account that you can transfer the funds back to. Ideally, you want this business account to be separate from your personal account for tax and accounting purposes.

Fortunately, getting an additional bank account typically isn't that complicated. You can set up a free checking account through a number of banks and it usually only takes about a week to process and get up and running. I've left a recommendation to secure a checking account for your business earlier in the book, but if you haven't completed this, you can still use your current account for testing purposes. Just be sure to have your new account ready before launch date.

Once you scale to the point where you will need an official business checking account, you can switch to some other banks if necessary, so don't spend too much effort choosing the perfect banking account early. Just make sure it's free and accepts electronic deposits from Stripe or Square.

Okay, so to recap this section: your goal is to set up your payment processing and run a test sale. Once everything is working, let's get started launching your offer.

SUMMARY OF THIS LESSON'S ACTION ITEMS:

- Set up a payment integration on your website and connect your bank account.
- Run a full set of test payments from A-Z making sure all the thank you emails and payment transfers get completed without errors. Take notes along the way and identify any friction points or questions a potential customer would have.

LESSON 19: THE SOFT LAUNCH

LESSON 19

LESSON 19 DETAILS

TIMELINE: DAY 21
ESTIMATED TIME TO COMPLETE: 60 MIN.

You've put in the effort in the previous chapters. You've built a powerful offer, you've created a beautiful sales page, you've researched your competition. You are ready for your soft launch. We don't need to get nervous thinking about the official launch yet. For now, we'll keep it within your friends and family. All you have to do for your soft launch is contact 20 of your close friends and family to tell them about what you're up to.

Oh, and to raise the stakes a little bit, I'll also challenge you to post two social media posts about your new business. You can do a story on Instagram or a photo of you and your cat with the caption:

'Guess who just started a business?!' or something fun. This is your icebreaker to the world. It doesn't have to be formal or overly complicated.

When you reach out to your friends and family, I would recommend a phone call or a direct text message. You're almost guaranteed that they will see it, read it, and reply because they know you already. Remember, these are your close friends and family — you're not pressuring them for a sale as much as you are asking them for their feedback and showing off your brand new baby.

If this feels awkward, here's a sample script you can use:

"Hey Johnny, I just decided to launch a side hustle where I do XYZ. It would mean a lot to me if you could check out my store and let me know any feedback you might have. Of course, if you need XYZ, I'll be more than happy to get you a special friend rate. Here's the link to my shop: [insert link]. Let me know what you think!"

The reason this text works so well is because you're not pressuring them to buy. The main ask is for feedback. It shows that you value their opinion and want them to be involved in something that you care about. They will actually feel honored that you are inviting them to take a peak. Now, you don't want to leave them only asking for feedback, because they might actually be interested in your service. By offering an invitation for them to shop with you, it lets them know that you're open for business.

You'll probably get a few good ideas and some suggestions from your friends. You might get a couple sales, and you might get some people that will get really excited and ask you to partner up with them. All of this stuff would never happen if you didn't reach out to them in the first place.

Now, you have your script, and you have 20 people in your contact list. It's time to start sending messages.

Here's the thing. I need you to be serious about this. I need you to make sure you don't stop at five friends or 10 friends. Make sure you go all the way up to 20. Is there a science behind it? Not really — just that most people are too scared to ask for help and are likely to avoid this out of fear. You're going to have to commit to putting yourself out there. Asking 20 people in your circle of friends is a very great way to warm up, build confidence, and gain momentum before launching your big campaign.

SUMMARY OF THIS LESSON'S ACTION ITEMS:

- Announce your offer to 20 of your friends and family. Present your offer as a soft launch and ask for their feedback.
- Make two posts on social media about your soft launch and monitor the comments. You can ask for feedback if you're feeling too shy to ask for a sale. (But you only get to be shy during the soft launch. In the next lesson, it's time to roll up your sleeves and be proud to share your new company!)

LESSON 20:
THE BIG LAUNCH

LESSON 20 DETAILS

Buckle your seatbelts folks, this rocketship is blasting off!

You're finally ready to tell the world about your offer and start getting customers!

Remember, it's important to think about what people are in the market for right now — the last thing you want to do is shove your offer down someone's throat if they're not ready to buy. Instead, focus on the value and the transformation that your product will provide.

But we've already gone through all that earlier. Now we just need to put your product in front of the right people.

Fundamentally, this is simple. When it actually comes time to do it, you're going to have to battle a barrage of excuses, self-doubts, criticism, fears, insecurities, and all kinds of imaginary reasons why "this idea isn't good enough." That's the real challenge. So many people (myself included) get stuck in launch paralysis. The act of building and preparing to launch is so fun and exciting, but when it comes time to actually push the button and do the work of announcing your offer to the world, everyone chickens out.

Why is that? Why is it so hard to simply flip the switch and start broadcasting your new company to the world?

There's usually one simple answer: fear of judgement.

Sometimes, it's not so simple.

Another challenge some people face is the avoidance of doing the work because their subconscious is afraid of change. They're forever trapped, enslaved by their own ego who is trying to protect them from potential dangers, even though doing nothing is far more dangerous in the long run.

Fortunately, the good news for both of these scenarios is really cut and dry. Do it anyway.

Up until now, you've been able to build so much momentum, you've done your research, you've polished and perfected your business model. You're ready to unveil your new project to the world. Remember, this is something your future customers need you to do. This is something your future self needs you to do.

You're going to have to push through the fears and follow this chapter step-by-step until at least 1,000 people have visited your sales page.

If you try everything in this book, and you still can't get 1,000 people to your sales page, then you have permission to scrap the idea, take the things you learned, and go back at it with a new idea — but you don't get to give up if you haven't tried. Trust me, I've done that so many times, and there's nothing more disheartening than knowing you gave up too early because you were too nervous about what people might think.

We don't have time to be concerned about what others might think right now. Either they will support your idea or they won't. No big deal.

Great. So now that that's out of the way, let's get started with the actual plan of how we're going to announce your big idea. We've already done a soft launch by texting 20 people.

To start things off, we're going to choose one to three of the promotion methods below that best represent where you will find your customer in their "natural habitat." Where are your people hanging out? Refer back to your customer development exercises.

If your target market is 50 year-old CEOs of financial tech companies, no matter how much money you spend advertising on Twitch, you're highly unlikely to find a customer on the platform because it is a platform for young gamers. That being said, Twitch might be a great place to advertise for an SAT Prep Course or a neon gaming keyboard.

Mission: Choose up to three promotion methods that your customers will resonate with. Consider the options below.

1. *Organic Social Media Posting*

   - Create valuable, shareable and consistent content for a social media channel. (Note: this takes time to grow at first. Your results will start to compound once you have an audience. You can speed up audience growth with some of the strategies in Lesson 28.)

     - Instagram
     - Pinterest
     - LinkedIn
     - Twitter
     - Facebook

2. *Paid Advertising (digital)*

   - Paid advertising is one of the fastest ways to get massive attention to your offer, but it comes at a price. If you have the capital and are familiar with building an ad campaign, this can be a fairly predictable way to get some initial impressions. It's a good idea to support your paid promotion efforts with more long term strategies like audience building. Building a business solely on paid ads will make it difficult to earn a profit in the long run. So if you do choose the paid channel, I would recommend balancing your effort with an organic channel as well to protect yourself in the long run.

3. *Advertising in Niche Specific Publications (industry news sites / community forums)*

- You can get some very hot leads by purchasing an advertisement in a niche website or publication. If you sell a gardening kit, you can contact gardening blogs or sites and purchase ads directly from the publisher. I often got great results buying ads on an acting site when selling video services to actors.

4. *Deal Sites (like Groupon or LivingSocial)*

- People on these sites are looking to buy. They have their wallet in their hand looking for a solution for their product. The only drawback here is that you're sharing a 50% chunk of the already discounted rate with the deal site. As long as you build your margin in and have room for upsells, these sites can bring you some great attention, and you don't have to pay anything up front. We'll have more on this in Lesson 23.

5. *Craigslist and Classifieds*

- Don't discount Craigslist. Yes, there are a lot of scammers out there, but there are also plenty of good customers looking for a great product. Your job is to figure out how to position your offer on the platform so you can attract the right buyer. I have a friend who posted photos of her paintings and tagged them as "original art - CB2 West Elm" and she got dozens of inquiries and a sale at $1,200 in the first week. You should know that even with getting a gallery to represent me, it took a lot of effort to sell a few of my own paintings at the same price. I also had to eat commission and marketing expenses. Craigslist was free to post, and she doesn't have to share a commission.

6. *Mining for Leads*

- If your customers are business owners or corporate contacts, you can research leads through LinkedIn and other business directories for their contact information. I've had some success in the past hiring a specialist from Fiverr to build a list, and then either contacting the list myself or hiring another specialist to do the outreach. It's

important to note, however, during times of economic downturn —
it's a lot harder to make cold outreach work. Business owners are less
interested in starting new deals or spending their money.

> ➤ Pay an email researcher on Fiverr (or do it yourself)
> ➤ Contact the leads directly via phone, on LinkedIn, or by email

7. *Use lead sites like Bark.com, Angi.com or Thumbtack to tap into a network of people looking for professional services.*

- These sites are fantastic for service-based businesses and provide dedicated platforms with plenty of visitors. These marketplaces make it easy to find clients and set your prices.

8. *Post in Forums / Community boards (respectfully)*

- Are you active on Reddit, Quora or another community board? You can use this to attract new customers by being helpful and providing value. Of course, don't ignore the rules of the community.

9. *Facebook Groups / Slack Groups / Discord Groups*

- Groups are a great place to communicate to a number of people in the community and get referrals. You want to be providing a very special deal or giving back in a way that benefits the community more than you if you want to see success here. Avoid "self promotion" tactics, and think about ways you can be of help if you want the group to respond with interest.

10. *Paid Partnerships / Influencer Marketing*

- You can use sites like TensorSocial or MightyScout to build a list of influencers in your niche with target audiences and then connect with influencers and ask them for a sponsorship rate.

11. *Produce a video show (YouTube)*

- Learning to develop YouTube is challenging. YouTube is extremely competitive and can take years to develop. That being said, if you get it right, YouTube can bring endless opportunities and loyal customers your way for years to come.

12. *Produce an audio show (podcast)*

- Audio is a lot easier to produce than video, and it's never been easier with tools like Anchor.fm. If you have a unique story or angle, you can start to build an audience through podcasting and have loyal customers lining up to buy from you in time. Like YouTube, this is a long term play. Don't expect overnight success. I've been involved in several podcasts through the years as a host and producer. Ultimately, a podcast can bring you extremely high quality leads over time.

13. *Publish a Blog or a Magazine (another long term play)*

- Raking in the site traffic from people who are searching Google for businesses that do what you do is a great way to build a stream of customers for the long haul. Every article you write can live online forever, compounding over time. Just as many streams make a river, you might not be able to reap the benefits of monetizing a blog early, but it can become extremely profitable down the road.

14. *Public Speaking (Either virtually or at local events)*

- One of the most powerful sales opportunities is through public speaking. If you are on stage you immediately garner a position of respect and authority, making people interested in what you have to say. Provide value and inspiration and you should be able to leverage opportunities through this channel.

15. *Affiliate Partnerships*

- Find someone with an audience and give them a cut in exchange for promotion. These partnerships should be a win-win for both parties, so think hard on how you can help the other party.

16. *Local Marketing*

- Flyers, newspapers, street teams, or direct mail brochures provide a reliable way to get the attention of locals. Sure, there's a lot of elbow grease with this method, but most people are too lazy to go this route. You might find less competition if you're creative and able to put in the hustle.

17. *Go Live (one of the most powerful forms of marketing in existence)*

- Want to grow even faster? Do a joint live with other hustlers and combine forces. With all the platforms like Instagram, Clubhouse, LinkedIn, YouTube, Twitch, etc. there's plenty of opportunity to connect live with people all over the world.

It's important to keep your focus intact. Don't try to do everything on this list at first. Choose no more than three channels to focus on.

Once you have your channels decided it's time to move to the next step in this mission: share your offer on the channels you chose! Get out there and make it happen.

You'll need to be extremely consistent. You can't just put out a paid ad for $10 and expect it to solve all of your problems. Keep swinging, stay positive, and know that it might take some experimentation before you get it right.

The goal is to keep promoting in the three channels you've selected until you get 1,000 people to see your offer, and ideally at least 100 people to visit your shop. During that time, you're going to keep refining your offer based on the feedback and data you get, but don't give up and don't slow down until you show 1,000 people your offer.

Getting 1,000 people to see a brand new offer can be challenging for a new product, but since your product is awesome, it will be a blast!

No matter the case, you might need to get some reinforcements or extra tactics to help you find the right buyers for your product — that's what the next section is all about.

SUMMARY OF THIS LESSON'S ACTION ITEMS:

- Choose three promotion channels to present your offer in. These three channels should represent the sweet spot between where the majority of your customers are visiting as well as where you're comfortable creating posts in. If you don't understand organic social media, maybe paid ads or local marketing is better for you. Choose the three channels that you feel will bring the best results.
- Double down on your promotion until you reach a minimum of 1,000 visitors to your sales page or shop.

PART 5
GET YOUR FIRST SALE

What is the difference between an idea and a revenue generating business? One sale.

You only need to get one sale to prove that your idea can become a business. Once you get that first sale, you can look at the steps you took to make that happen and start to replicate them until sales happen more frequently, and more predictably. That's the game of business.

In Part 6, we're going to discuss some wildly unorthodox methods to push through whatever roadblocks are keeping you from crossing the threshold between zero sales and one sale. The lessons after that are about how to scale beyond that first sale and optimize for long term success.

Now, you may have already achieved a sale during your big announcement. That's wonderful! The strategies in the next few lessons are all about accelerating results. You may choose to use these strategies when you need to increase your exposure and reach. Think of these as bonus levers you can pull to get more customers in the door.

The four lessons in Part 6 will revolve around the following topics:

1. Recruiting help from your network to give your campaign a boost.
2. Setting up a sale to create a flood of new customers.
3. Harnessing the power of deal sites and other resources to get your marketing out there.
4. How to use DMs and text messages to rally additional support.

LESSON 21: RECRUIT HELP

LESSON 21 DETAILS

It takes an army.

You are rewriting the story of the world around you. You're not only building a new source of employment for yourself — one that didn't exist before you started creating it — you're building a new force that is interacting with the world around you, too.

Your efforts are not being performed in a vacuum. When you order supplies, it helps other side hustlers. When you improve the lives of your customers, they accomplish more things and maybe start their own businesses.

With that being said, why should you go it alone?

You're going to need help. There are so many people out there who are looking for someone to simply ASK for their help. I can't stress this enough. People love to help. People love to be involved in something proactive. You'll get there so much faster if you ask.

If the friends you ask don't have the time to help at the level you need, that's fine — keep asking until you find the right people.

Your mission in this chapter is to approach 10 friends or mentors and ask for advice or assistance in getting sales for your offer. I would recommend asking people who either run their own business or are involved in the marketing of another business. If you don't have 10 friends in your circle, you can join my mastermind group for some peer support. Just email me at noah@startbrigade.com for details.

Once you approach 10 people, ask them for two things: their feedback and their support. Feedback is important. You'll get an outside perspective to look at your business and give you their recommendations on what you should do. This is advice from people who have been there before, done this already. You won't be able to do EVERYTHING that your mentors recommend, but if you implement even one recommendation that pays off, you're on the right track.

Support is another really important part of this lesson. You'll be surprised at how fast you can grow when collaborating with other businesses. Support can take many forms from collaborating on a webinar to sharing retail space — and each mentor you approach might have a different resource to contribute.

When asking for support and feedback, tell them what your challenge is, show them your current offer and talk to them about your current promotion strategy. Come from a place of humility and show them your enthusiasm.

When it comes to feedback, these insights will come in handy for the next few months. You'll want a place to document this feedback for reference later. **As you get the feedback and advice from your mentors or peers, it will help to categorize the suggestions into three types of feedback:**

1. Attention and Acquisition Feedback
2. Conversion Feedback
3. Product and Pricing Feedback

Ultimately, you're looking for actionable adjustments you can implement to boost your sales and revenue. **There are fundamentally three levers you can pull to get more business:**

1. The number of people who see your offer
2. The percentage of those people who convert to a sale
3. The price that you sell at

Organizing the feedback based on these categories will help you to choose which strategies to implement next. If you are strong in Acquisition (number of people who see your offer) but weak in conversions (getting visitors to make a purchase) then it would make sense to focus on the advice around conversions and ignore the acquisition recommendations until you are ready to implement.

It might also be a good idea to group the support from your peers and mentors into categories as well. For example, John has a big social media following and he will help promote you. John's support would be related to the acquisition category. Maybe another friend, Rosy, offers to design some professional images for your website and sales page. Her support would be related to conversions.

It might be tempting to try to go it alone and prove that you can do this, but you're going to have to shift this mentality to one of growing together. You've got big dreams. You can't get there alone. You're an incredible individual, and you're destined for greatness. Ask your friends and mentors for help getting there. You never know how powerful you'll become together. Just ask.

SUMMARY OF THIS LESSON'S ACTION ITEMS:

- Approach 10 trusted friends, peers, or mentors to ask for advice on how you can improve your offer and your promotion. As always, if you don't have any mentors you can approach, you are welcome to schedule a strategy call with me on my website.
- Categorize the feedback you receive and create an action plan to implement the highest leverage activities.

LESSON 22: THE POWER OF THE SALE

LESSON 22 DETAILS

TIMELINE: DAY 26–27
ESTIMATED TIME TO COMPLETE: 60 MIN.

Sometimes your customers just need a little push to spend money on your product. Maybe they don't urgently need your offer right now, so they're just considering purchasing it one day in the distant future (which really means they're going to forget all about it and buy someone else's offer eventually). So how do you give them a little nudge in the right direction, without making them feel pressured?

Make your offer too good to last. Give them a deal so amazing they feel compelled to pull their wallet out right now and pay. There's real magic in a limited time sale. If you give your customer an exclusive time bound opportunity to save big, they're much more likely to feel like they're making the right choice to spend now.

In marketing, you're not only trying to put a good product in front of a customer who desires it, but you're aiming to make that desire overcome any objections the customer might have to purchasing it as well. As the customer is going through their decision making process, they're subconsciously weighing the pros and cons of making the purchase. So what do you think happens when you put a very lucrative deal that expires soon in front of a customer who is making a decision? They'll start telling themselves all the reasons they should buy the product now. The objections the customer is considering begin to switch from all the reasons they shouldn't buy the product to all the things they will miss out on if they don't buy now.

These strategies are great to deploy once in a while to boost attention and get solid leads, but you should be careful not to be completely dependent on them. Ever drive past a "grand opening sale" sign that has been plastered on a shop for 3 years? Eventually, you'll have to take your sale down and build a solid stream of non-sale revenue.

What are the key points of a great deal?

A great deal is limited to a short time frame. If you're launching a sale, keep it limited, and keep it focused. If your customers know that the sale is gone in 24 hours, never to come back, they'll be much more inclined to take action and snag the deal. If they know the deal isn't going anywhere, there's no reason for them to take their wallets out now. They'll just keep browsing. Give them a reason to buy today, right now.

A great deal is simple and specific. You want to draw the customer in with a very simple to understand value. Confusing deals and red tape slow down the decision making process. Don't add friction by making your deal confusing. If you have several deals presented on the same banner or offer, the customer will feel overwhelmed and not know which deal to focus on. Don't let your deals cannibalize each other. A great deal is something like "50% off all rentals in July!" It's clear, time bound, and specific.

A great deal is also highly visible. Don't be bashful of your special deal. Put it out in front where your customers can see it. If you're afraid that the customer might actually purchase the deal, consider reworking the incentive until you feel comfortable about selling it.

SUMMARY OF THIS LESSON'S ACTION ITEMS:

- Create a very irresistible deal or sale and announce it to your customers. Think about your promotion channels from your launch plan and make sure you are announcing your sale on every one of your established channels.
- Be sure to include the three key points of a good deal in the construction of your sale and have them apparent in the description:
  - ▷ Keep it limited to a time bound offer
  - ▷ Keep it simple and specific
  - ▷ Make it visible

LESSON 23:
LEVERAGING DEAL
SITES, AFFILIATES,
JOINT VENTURES

LESSON 23 DETAILS

Alright so maybe there's a chance that even with your limited time sale, you're still not getting customers rolling in. Have no fear, you still have plenty of other cards up your sleeve. In this lesson we'll go over some powerful resources you can put into action that let you leverage other people's networks to get more sales.

When you're just starting out, resources are slim. So, with that in mind, our criteria for this lesson is to focus on resources that don't come with massive upfront costs like paid advertising. Although this chapter doesn't include every strategy and resource under the sun, we'll focus on three types of partnerships that you can take advantage of to kick start sales for your business.

The three types of partnerships we'll go over are:

1. Deal sites
2. Affiliates
3. Joint Ventures.

Deal Sites

Deal sites are great for injecting cash into your business early on and getting some customers on the radar. Because you'll be sharing profits AND offering a deal, you probably won't be making as much in profit, but you can potentially recover that setback through volume.

Groupon and other deal sites allow you to leverage customers who are ready to make a purchase. You'll be able to present a great offer to more people without spending any money on advertising. These sites have built in audiences and powerful visibility on search engines. You can attract some attention quickly with the right deal.

Be careful to structure your deal in a way that you'll actually make money though. The deal sites often take a 50% cut of every sale, and expect that you provide a compelling enough sale on top of that. Ultimately, that means you'll be out a big chunk of your profit. If this is still cheaper than what it costs to run paid advertising, then it's worth looking into.

Groupon is probably the most universal deal site, but you can also find some niche specific deal sites that will have even more hyper targeted results. AppSumo is a deal site specifically for software and digital goods with a very strong network. We ran a couple deals through them at the agency I worked with, and I was thoroughly impressed with the attention to detail in the operation at AppSumo. Pay attention to the terms and make sure that the return is still going to be worth it for you. The deal sites also expect to make money from your offer.

Affiliates

We've all heard of affiliate marketing, and some might even have a negative impression of it. But affiliate marketing is still a very powerful method of marketing. Think back to a time you were doing research for which computer to buy, or what travel destination to go to. Chances are, you stumbled across a very well written blog or YouTube video reviewing the choices. Guess what, if you clicked one of the recommendations in that review and made a purchase, you just used affiliate marketing!

You can use affiliates to have other marketing experts promote your product for you and give them a commission. Most of these marketing experts already have websites, mailing lists or YouTube audiences that they occasionally recommend great products to. Every time they make a recommendation, they get commission.

So how can you enlist these affiliate marketers to your cause?

Amazon Affiliates is the most popular affiliate program and works primarily for physical products. Clickbank is another one of the more popular sites to set up an affiliate program as a seller. You simply upload your offer, assets and information to the site and interested affiliates can choose to direct their audience to your offer.

There are many other sites out there, but you certainly want to do your research. If you do go with an affiliate program, you'll have to create a funnel and make sure everything is turn-key and operational for the affiliate marketers. The more dialed in your funnel and landing page are, the easier it will be for the affiliates to earn commission, so they will be more likely to push your product with the maximum gusto!

You can also find affiliates through offering a program on your website for existing customers or colleagues. The more attractive your offer, the more exciting it will be for an affiliate to latch on to it and start promoting.

Joint Ventures

Finally, you can do some direct outreach to people who have a similar audience and do a joint venture. If you create very favorable commission terms, you can use the audience and marketing of an existing company to do sales for you. You would simply give a cut to the partner.

As your network expands and your product offering matures, you'll find more and more opportunities for joint Ventures.

SUMMARY OF THIS LESSON'S ACTION ITEMS:

- Research a few deal sites and affiliate sites and evaluate whether going this route will work for your business.
- If you do decide to implement one of these strategies, perform the napkin math to estimate how much you will be discounting your offer and what profit you will be making from the deal overall.
- Finally, make sure you are ready to fulfill the orders. If you get a huge influx of orders, you'll need to be able to deliver.

LESSON 24:
SLIDING INTO THE DM

LESSON 24 DETAILS

TIMELINE: DAY 29
ESTIMATED TIME TO COMPLETE: 30–90 MIN.

Don't underestimate chat marketing. The text message or DM is one of the most powerful tools you have at your fingertips to get your offer out there. If you're having any resistance getting your first few sales in the door, nothing will help you break through faster than sending direct messages to people you already have a relationship with.

The trick is to not be spammy about it. If you haven't spoken to your friend in three years and you suddenly text out the blue asking if he wants to pay you to teach him guitar he might be surprised. Now if you've already had a conversation going, it becomes much easier to drop in your offer and float it by them.

To help you craft your direct message, let's think about what that perfect text message should look like.

A great (non-spammy) text message should:

- Be genuine.
- Be concise. No one likes walls of text.
- Be clear. Tell them that you have an offer and give them the next step if they are interested in moving forward.

- Be respectful. Enough said.
- Give an out. Let them also reply back to say hello if they don't want to buy.

Example:

Hey John, I just started a new hustle! I'm officially doing ____ to help you ____.
I was actually pretty nervous to launch, but here we are!
If it's something you'd be interested in let's chat!
Of course, no pressure. Would also be great to simply connect and hear how things are going/chat about other projects.

SUMMARY OF THIS LESSON'S ACTION ITEMS:

- Draft a genuine, non-spammy direct message and send it to 20 people you know who might be interested in your product.
- Ask them for their business directly, or ask if they know of someone who might be interested. Don't be shy!

TIP:

You might find yourself writing many custom emails and responses to people saying the same thing over and over again.

You can save yourself hours and hours by saving these responses in templates on your email signature or as keystroke commands that will automatically unfurl a template when you type a set of commands.

You can set up automatic text expansion through premium tools like TextExpander as well as manually setting shortcuts in your keyboard settings. TextExpander is premium. Adjusting your keyboard settings and storing shortcuts is free. Setting up your email signature templates in your email client is also typically free. Choose the method that you prefer and enjoy having your frequently typed responses magically appear on the screen.

PART 6

SETTING YOUR NEW BUSINESS UP FOR LONG TERM SUCCESS

Up until now, everything has been culminating on getting your business launched and out of the gate.

However, your job doesn't stop at the launch.

Even if it were a race to some arbitrary finish line, a true race is never decided by the starting line. You have to be prepared for the long haul.

The following lessons are meant to provide you a foundation for setting up a business that can weather the tides of time and scale.

Granted, these are long term solutions that you may still be working on months after you launch your business. I will attempt to write them in a similar style as the previous chapters with actionable steps that you can do in each lesson. That being said, some things might require your business to be further along than is possible in a 30 day timeline (especially if you still have a full time job)

In the following eight lessons and activities you'll be acquiring the foundations and a roadmap that you can apply to scaling when you are ready.

LESSON 25:
LEARNING TO DELEGATE FOR LONG LASTING FREEDOM

LESSON 25

UP UNTIL NOW, YOU'VE PROBABLY BEEN DOING A LOT OF THE 'WORK' ON YOUR OWN.

YOUR NEW 'SIDE HUSTLE' MIGHT EVEN BE STARTING TO FEEL LIKE A SECOND JOB...

FROM THIS POINT ON, THE FOCUS IS TO TAKE THE HUSTLE OFF YOUR PLATE, AND TO INTRODUCE PEOPLE AND SYSTEMS THAT CAN DO THE WORK FOR YOU --

-- ACROSS THE ENTIRE CHAIN OF YOUR BUSINESS.

FINDING A TEAM WHO CAN DO ALL THE WORK YOU'RE DOING MIGHT SOUND LIKE GETTING A WISH FROM A GENIE'S LAMP

BUT DON'T GET INTIMIDATED! IT'S ENTIRELY POSSIBLE.

LIKE EVERYTHING, WE JUST NEED TO APPROACH IT ONE STEP AT A TIME.

STEP 1 IS TO WRITE DOWN A MASTER LIST OF ALL THE TASKS YOU ACTUALLY DO IN YOUR DAY TO DAY.

STEP 2 IS TO THINK ABOUT WHICH COMPONENTS AND TASKS YOU CAN OFFLOAD TO AN ASSISTANT, CONTRACTOR, OR SPECIALIST.

STEP 3 IS TO CREATE THE INSTRUCTIONS FOR YOUR NEW ASSISTANT TO FOLLOW. (YOU CAN DO SCREEN RECORDED VIDEOS)

AND STEP 4 IS TO HIRE, TRAIN, AND EMPOWER YOUR ASSISTANT TO DO THEIR NEW JOB!

THE BEST SIDE HUSTLES DON'T REQUIRE MUCH WORK WHEN THEY'RE UP AND RUNNING.

YOUR MISSION IN THIS LESSON IS TO TAKE THE FIRST STEP IN OFFLOADING YOUR 'HUSTLE' BY HIRING ONE PART TIME ASSISTANT TO DO AT LEAST ONE ASPECT OF YOUR BUSINESS.

TODAY'S MISSION

READY? GO!

LESSON 25 DETAILS

Earlier in the book, when we were going through deciding which business idea to focus on, one of the criteria was that it should be something that can eventually be scaled. What that means is that it is capable of generating revenue without trading time for money. You want a business, not a second job.

In this lesson, we're going to discuss a few strategies that can liberate you from the clock and start to build an operation that not only runs by itself, but grows over time. You'll systematically replace your time and labor with operators, systems, and workflows. In this lesson we'll discuss a bit of each of these, but the main focus is on the operators.

It's no secret that one of the most powerful resources a business can employ on the path to scaling is delegating work to great people. But when is the right time to hire someone in your business? Should you wait until you are cash flow positive? Should you wait until you get a fancy award and now feel like you are worthy to hire people? Of course not. The best time to hire help is NOW. Whether it's a virtual assistant or a contractor to handle specific tasks, the sooner you start to offload projects, the sooner you will be free to scale.

Delegation truly is your ultimate super power as a business owner, and if you cultivate this skill ruthlessly, not only will you reduce your workload, but you'll free yourself up to expand the business. You will also develop better systems for delegating through practice, and the skills of your team will grow, enabling them to achieve more alongside you.

Personally, I recommend starting your delegation practice with hiring a virtual assistant. Finding a great virtual assistant can literally be game changing. You can start with as little as 10 hours a month to handle some of the more tedious tasks that you find yourself doing, and then add on more when you're ready. The goal is to consistently move towards delegating everything in your business in time. Alright, so you're probably wondering how to go find one of these magical virtual assistants and start doing less drudgery.

Let's go ahead and cover the basic process for identifying which tasks to delegate, how to hire a virtual assistant, and how to train your team. I've developed a more in depth process on how to delegate like a champion in one of my online courses that you can purchase from my website at www.startbrigade.com.

In order to delegate your tasks like a pro there's a simple 5 step process to follow. **These 5 steps will build the foundations for scaling and once you have them implemented across every layer of your business you'll be well on your way to exponential growth.**

1. Make a list of the typical responsibilities you have in your business.
2. Next, list out all the tasks (components and actions) that make up each responsibility.
3. Then, beside each task, make a note on whether or not you could potentially train someone else to handle that specific task.
4. For the tasks that can be delegated, make a training video describing how to do the task (or how you want the task done if it's not your expertise).
5. Then, find someone through job boards, Fiverr, or personal connections to do the task at a fair rate.

SUMMARY OF THIS LESSON'S ACTION ITEMS:

- Go through steps one and two on the five step delegation exercise to create a list of all the tasks you do on a daily basis.
- From there, choose your single most time consuming, important, or frustrating task and create a training document or video outlining the steps involved.
- Finally, research someone on Fiverr or hire a part time assistant to do the task as specified in your brief.

TIP:

If you're looking to hire your first virtual assistant, I would suggest checking out a company called MyCloudCrew[3]. They're based in the Philippines and have some very well trained talent. At the time of writing I have two assistants through them and am constantly impressed with their attention to detail and professionalism.

Once you're established and have the budget for US based talent, check out Belay staffing to find very experienced and capable assistants.

---

3   https://mycloudcrew.com/

LESSON 26:
ALWAYS BE TESTING

LESSON 26 DETAILS

Business is always going to be dynamic. You're never completely finished optimizing and improving your operation.

One important question you might be wondering is, "If it's already working, why on earth do you need to spend time and energy testing and improving it?"

There's not one single answer to this question, there's actually three answers!

First, you can bet your bottom dollar that your competition will always be improving their products and offerings. If you fall asleep at the wheel and get complacent, some other entrepreneur will come along and outprice you or outperform you.

Second, the needs of the customer will always be evolving. With the dynamic times we live, you can imagine your customers will change their behaviors and buying patterns frequently. You'll need to run experiments and gather feedback to keep your offer relevant.

Third, the work on perfecting your product, people, systems and culture are never done. If you adopt a habit of experimentation, you'll be positioned to make massive improvements on your own product without waiting for external feedback from customers or competition.

Experimentation is where real innovation comes from. But experimentation can also be expensive. You can find something that can radically change your business, but if you're not systematic with your experiments, you can easily lose focus and chase the latest fad without focusing on what's working.

How many tests should you run, and how much effort should you spend on experimenting with out of the box ideas? Although not set in stone, you should anticipate spending 80 to 90 percent of your effort on the part of your business that is already working. Then you can use the remaining 10 to 20 percent for experimentation.

When you're trying something new, it's also important to give it a predetermined run time. You don't want to drag out a failing experiment for too long, or give up too early on a possible winner. As long as you are giving yourself adequate time to see a test through, you should be fine. Remember, there are whole teams at big companies specifically devoted to testing and experimentation. Be aware of your limitations, and don't try to bite off more than you can chew. It's enough that you adopt a habit of documenting your experiments, and keeping at least one active test running at a time.

A Quick Guide on How to Run Tests

Testing used to be something I would do based on feelings. I would hear about some new strategy or fad, and then stop everything to try it out. After pouring in a bunch of energy and finances, the new project would end up being a dud, and I would have to go back to my original plan. I'm sure you can imagine how demoralizing that can be.

I almost destroyed one business because I had decided to go "all in" on a virtual reality fad that cost me thousands of dollars in cash as well as a huge chunk of time being sidetracked from my core business. It wouldn't be until a couple years later that I would learn a simple process for running calculated experiments that can bring consistent improvements and innovation without gambling the house away. I learned this process from my former manager and friend Zach Grove while working at Single Grain.

As long as you have a great process in place, it's okay to take some risks and try some out of the box ideas. Below you will find a six step process for running and maintaining tests as you grow your business. You'll want to bookmark this and come back to it as you need it.

Step 1: Prepare an easy to access list of resources for inspiration.

You'll find ideas for things to test based on your past results. If something worked, there's probably something you can do to either duplicate it or optimize it. You can also look at your competitors and the campaigns or programs they are releasing. Finally, you can look for inspiration in publications about your specific niche or industry. Keep this list easy to access and to add to. You can use a Google Doc or Notion document and bookmark the link in a folder on your browser.

Key sources to find inspiration:

1. Your past successes.
2. Your competitors' and peers' initiatives.
3. Knowledge from industry news and training programs.

Step 2: Create a place to list tests.

You'll want to keep track of your experiments in a consistent fashion. You don't need to overwhelm yourself with data, so a simple Google Sheet or Excel spreadsheet will work just fine. You can use the following columns in your spreadsheet:

- A short description of the test
- Your expected results (hypothesis)
- The start and end dates
- The ending results

Set a recurring calendar block once a week or so to update this sheet. If you want to tie your experiments with a task manager and assign due dates to different actions, you can opt to use a kanban board in Asana or Trello. These kanban boards have cards or tasks lined up and you can move them across different columns to track progress.

To keep yourself from being overwhelmed, you should only have a handful of tests running at a time. You can put your upcoming test ideas in a queue and run them in order of priority and impact as soon as you have bandwidth available for more testing.

Step 3: Pick a desired channel or outcome to test.

You can categorize your outcomes based on impact to categories like these:

- Sales / lead generation pipeline
- Marketing and branding
- Your product or service
- Recruitment and hiring
- Automation, systems and scaling

You can also get even more granular and test a specific lever within each category. For example, you can run one test to measure the effect of an ad for getting more cold traffic (acquisition) to a sales page, and another test to measure how a landing page performs if you change the copy (conversion).

Step 4: Create a hypothesis.

This doesn't have to be a complicated statement, in fact, the more simple it is, the better. Your hypothesis should simply state "because I see 'X' (past data, competition, industry news), I expect 'Y' to occur if I do 'Z.'"

Where 'Y' is some quantifiable number tied to your desired channel or outcome and 'Z' is the test you perform.

For example: "Because I see Sam's Dog Grooming hiring influencers to promote their service consistently, I expect a 50% increase in sales if I hire five influencers to promote my handmade dog leashes this month."

Another example: "Because I saw a 30% increase in conversions when I mentioned a discount on the checkout page, I expect to see a similar 30% increase in click through rate on my advertisement if I mention the discount."

Step 5: Set your testing allowance.

Before you go and pour all your energy and budget into a new test, you'll need to predermine how much time, money, and effort goes into this test. Say you want to test if Facebook ads will bring you new sales. You might choose to run the test for 3 weeks and spend $500 / week.

Setting an allowance will keep you from burning out or burning your cash.

Step 6: Measure the results and call it a win or loss.

At the end of your predetermined time period or budget, it's time to look at the test results. Here is where you need to adopt an empirical mindset.

Either the test was a winner and you will adopt it into your regular business practices, or it was a loser and you will scrap it or adjust the parameters enough to test again. What you DON'T want to do is to continue the test if you already have enough data to determine a losing result.

Mark the results on your tracking sheet, and move your next experiment up in the queue.

If you are building a habit of testing and measuring each facet of your business, you are bound to keep moving in the right direction. Stick with it, and don't get complacent.

Now that we talked about the importance of experiments, your next mission is to perform step one and compile a starting list of inspiration resources. From there, set aside a recurring 30 minute slot on your calendar to think about what tests you can run in your business and measure the results of your active tests.

SUMMARY OF THIS LESSON'S ACTION ITEMS:

- Begin compiling your first lists of inspiration resources. These can be snippets of your past successes, screenshots of your competition, or a summary of a cool program you watched.
- Create a spreadsheet for tracking your next experiments.
- Set a recurring calendar block to spend 30 minutes thinking about your next experiments and measuring the results.

TIP:

Did you know you can use your phone as a personal secretary? Any time you have a great idea, you can use your phone as a place to quickly capture the cool idea so you can experiment with it later.

My favorite combination of apps and voice commands to capture random ideas or thoughts throughout the day is the reminders app and Siri on the iPhone. Android's Voice Access also has similar functions.

My script sounds like this: "Hey Siri, remind me to experiment with a newsletter like The Daily Stoic."

I then put my phone away and I can trust Siri to automatically add the note to the main list in the reminders app. I'll then go through every morning and organize the new reminders to individual lists or tasks on the calendar.

You can also geo-tag reminders or set them to trigger at a specific time on the calendar. And of course, you can turn Siri's audio responses off to speed your process up and avoid disturbing others in the room.

LESSON 27: CREATE YOUR HIRING ROADMAP

LESSON 27 DETAILS

The life of a business owner can sometimes feel like a game of whack-a-mole, where you're constantly bouncing around from one issue to the next.

As soon as you solve one problem, two more show up. You will always have customers who need your attention, employees or vendors who have unexpected schedule changes, and the unforeseen and unavoidable physical challenges of being a human in modern society.

The good news is that there's a way out of the whack-a-mole game. Actually, there are two ways: people and process.

Let's think about it. What happens if you get sick? Will the business continue to thrive without you? Unless you've invested in training a team and building repeatable systems that run on autopilot, probably not. More than that, if the business needs you to constantly perform the functions integral to its survival, eventually you will make a mistake. No matter how talented and smart you are, you're still human. You're going to get burned out.

It's time to start thinking about how to build a margin of safety so that your business doesn't go up in smoke if you step away.

To put it another way, the thing that will keep your business running without you is *leverage*.

Leverage is the ability to get the maximum amount of benefit out of something. Once you start to hire great people, you will effectively multiply your impact without spending more of your own hours in the business. That's leverage. Systems, templates, software, and experience can all be facets of leverage in your business.

If you build a system that automates your customer support replies, you're now able to enjoy the benefits of having your incoming support emails responded to efficiently without having to compose the replies on your own. Now, in our game of whack-a-mole, whenever the customer support mole pops up, you can sit back and relax because you have a trusty system that's handling it for you in the background.

There's no magic potion here, but fortunately the secret to fixing all these issues is a very simple methodology: one job at a time.

This lesson isn't about snapping your fingers and having all of your daily responsibilities offloaded to a team overnight. Rather, we're mapping out the future and planning which roles you should be looking to hire *eventually*.

You can use something called an organizational chart to map out the roles that you'll need to hire as you grow your business and fill it out by following these simple steps below.

1. First, you'll want to start by making a list of all the things that will happen in your business on a daily basis.
2. Next, you'll want to group these tasks and actions up by department type. *For example, invoicing clients and paying vendors might be encompassed in an accounting team.*
3. From there you'll decide how many jobs or people you'll need in each team to accomplish all the tasks. *For example, a digital creative team might have a graphic designer, copywriter and a website developer on the roster.*

4. Write each position's role on the organizational chart with a box or square around it.
5. Now, assign each team a manager or leader, and draw a line connecting the manager to each of the team members in their department.
6. If it makes sense, you'll want to give your managers a leader, or connect them straight to the CEO.
7. Depending on the complexity or size of a team, you might end up with vice presidents (VPs) of different departments like sales, operations, marketing, and product development who report to the CEO. And of course the managers of the different teams who report to the VPs.
8. To complete your first organization chart, go ahead and assign a name next to each job. At the beginning, all of these names might be YOUR name, and that's okay. In time, you'll start to recruit people for each job as you grow until eventually you're only responsible for one job.

After you've built your organizational chart, it's time to start making a plan to remove yourself from being responsible for every job and hire smart, capable experts to take charge of these roles. Most likely, you can only afford to hire one or two positions at a time. So, which position is the most urgent? Generally speaking, a position you should put highest in your priority for offloading will have some or all of the following characteristics:

1. It takes up a large portion of your time you should be spending in other areas.
2. You're not skilled or experienced at the job.
3. You're losing revenue because you don't have this role filled.
4. You dislike/dread doing the job.

If a particular job scores high on all four of these factors, then it should be one of the first jobs to find a replacement. I won't get into details on how to hire as that process extends well beyond the timeline set forth in this book. Instead, your mission in this lesson is to simply identify the roles that you will eventually need to hire and then rate them in order of priority to be delegated or automated. The clarity of a good hiring strategy will help you see the light at the end of the tunnel when things get tough.

SUMMARY OF THIS LESSON'S ACTION ITEMS:

- Your mission in this section is to pull out a notebook and pen and start documenting all the tasks you do on a daily basis.
- From there, organize your list of tasks into jobs on an organizational chart. Group similar jobs together in a department and give each department a manager. Have the managers report to a chief.
- Finally, number each job in order of urgency to be delegated or automated. The more detailed you are, the better. Eventually everything on the list can be handed off, increasing your leverage and freeing you up for the next level of business.

TIP:

As your business continues to grow, new tasks and jobs will show up that you or your team will be responsible for, and you'll have to continue to create new roles and then hire additional skilled talent to take your business to the next level.

- ▷ Things can get pretty complicated as you build out your team. You'll find yourself needing to repeat the same hiring processes over and over again and will want to have them streamlined. With that in mind, I've made a list of some helpful tools and resources to help keep track of your systems, processes and general organization.
- ▷ **Notion:** Works great as a wiki for processes. As you do tasks repeatedly, you can create a process document to hand off to your replacement when the time is right. Organize all the 'how-to' files in one place with Notion.
- ▷ **Airtable:** In my experience, this is the *crème de la crème* in database tools. Can be as simple or robust as you need to organize data, people, and projects.

- ▷ **Asana, Trello, Monday, or Wrike**: Great for task management and team management. (My favorite is Asana.)
- ▷ **HubSpot**: Great for organizing your customers and sales information.
- ▷ **G-Suite**: You can do wonders with spreadsheets that link to folders containing resources and supplementary files.
- ▷ **Loom**: Very easy screen record software for making quick instructional videos on the fly. Great for instructing a new assistant on how to perform tasks.
- ▷ **Fiverr**: When starting a new venture, almost all of my tasks are first delegated on Fiverr. I will use a specialist to test out a new process, and use the instructions I send to them as a template for future projects. Once I have things figured out on Fiverr, I'll either continue working with that contractor or hire someone to fill the role permanently.
- ▷ **MixMax, Drip, or MailChimp**: You'll need your emails to be automated eventually. There are dozens of email services that can handle automated outreach and newsletter servicing. You can also set up your new hire onboarding information in a daily email campaign for new hires to complete.
- ▷ **Zapier**: Once you start mixing all this software together, you might look into setting up some basic Zapier integrations that automatically fire actions based on triggers or events between apps. It can get complicated, so you might want to get some help from a developer when you're ready for this.

LESSON 28: BUILDING AN AUDIENCE FOR THE LONG HAUL

LESSON 28 DETAILS

Out of all the levers you can pull to grow your business for the long term, there is one that stands out as a truly exponential resource: audience building. An audience is, to put it simply, a group of individuals who follow your journey and subscribe to the media you share with them. Your audience can be diehard fans who hang on your every word and share every post you make on social media. Or they can be repeat buyers who are subscribed to your newsletter and purchase one of your offers every now and then.

Let's think about this: why is having an audience important? Today's market isn't just flooded with competition, it's flooded with information, distractions, shiny objects, and new trends that fly by us seemingly at the speed of light. If you're going to capture the attention of your customers, you're going to have to do something to stand out from all this chatter.

Television, Facebook, and Google have known about this since the early days: whoever controls the attention controls the revenue. If you have attention on your platform you can sell a portion of that to businesses and brands who want to reach the users on the platform. As a business using advertising to connect with customers, you're ultimately renting attention from the other guys.

If you've built an audience, you're able to sell products directly to a loyal customer base rather than working to attract new leads for every sale. Once you get the audience large enough, you're able to skip advertising altogether. The best part is that the customers who come from your media and content will already be familiar with your message and story, making it easier to convert them to a sale when the time is right.

Alright so who should build an audience? I get it, not everyone is a natural YouTube personality. But the beauty of media is that there are infinite ways to create content. You don't have to be a supermodel or a smooth talking video guru. You can just be you, and you can use a number of media outlets from the written word, audio, and video. You can even hire someone to be the face of your brand.

For this lesson, your mission is to decide on the style of audience you will deploy for your business and formulate an action plan that you can begin to execute on as you grow your business. This book is not the one that will guide you through your entire audience building path. We are simply laying the foundation in these chapters and giving you enough direction to get started when you're done with the book. If you want additional course corrections and advice for the later stages of audience development, visit my website and I'll point you to some additional resources and training.

Below, you will find a basic six step roadmap for building an audience. I'll also include a worksheet that you can download in the resources section of my website so you can create your audience building strategy. The actual assignment in this lesson is only to formulate your plan. Building an audience is a lifelong process.

Audience Building Step 1:
Choose your channel.

Double down on one core channel at the beginning and then expand once you have things spinning. Trying to do too many things at once is a recipe for disaster. Eventually, you will need to get your offer to every channel possible, but when you're starting out, focus on one.

Think about your strengths when choosing a channel:

- If you are a great writer, consider building a blog or magazine.
- If you're strong with video, maybe start with a YouTube channel.
- Podcasting is another great method to grow an audience and present your offer — it's also much easier than video to get started with.
- Instagram, TikTok, LinkedIn, or Clubhouse could be other great places to start.

Audience Building Step 2:
Decide your point of differentiation.

There are many ways to establish a point of differentiation:

- You can do daily shows
- You can interview interesting people.
- You can do a narrative story.
- The point of differentiation can be anything from the format to the actual content.
- It can even be as simple as your personality.

Audience Building Step 3:
Decide your release cadence and schedule.

Once you pick your channel and you find your point of differentiation, the next step is to determine how frequently you will publish your content. There are two schools of thought on how frequently you should publish.

One says publish daily and focus on shorter, more agile types of content around a specific topic. The other school of thought focuses on publishing less frequently while creating truly remarkable content. This could be something like a monthly magazine, or a monthly documentary series. The amount of effort put into a magazine can be much greater than a five minute podcast episode for example. Decide your format and stick with it.

Audience Building Step 4:
Prepare for a long battle.

Whatever release style you choose, get prepared to buckle in for at least six months with consistent publishing before you 'figure it out'. Resolve yourself now. It will become easier if you think of this process as a part of your new identity as the evangelist for your company. Some of you might be naturally gifted and will get it right on the first episode. Others might really struggle and not find their rhythm until eight or nine months in.

Keep at it, stay positive, and don't give up. Audience building is a long game. You don't get to just do it once and quit.

Audience Building Step 5:
Produce your pilot.

Start with about three to four weeks of content already completed and produced as a contingency before you start releasing. This way, you'll have a buffer of content ready to deploy as you get your bearings and get used to the habit of publishing.

It may be tempting to start releasing your content as soon as you have the first episodes complete, but if you run into a roadblock and you skip a few releases, it will be hard to get back into the routine. This extra buffer will keep you protected from some unforeseen setbacks and give you enough wiggle room to catch up with your release schedule if you slip a bit along the way.

Audience Building Step 6:
Start releasing your content.

At first, you are going to grow your main channel, and in time, you can expand to other platforms and channels. You'll want to tap into promotion strategies and make sure you're getting your content out to the world as best you can. Once you build momentum, you can start expanding your promotion efforts and adding more people to your content team.

Audience Building Step 7:
Keep going... but hire coaches along the way.

Stick with it. Investing in an audience is a lot like investing in a 401K. Keep making small deposits over time and eventually you'll start to get compounding interest and growth over time. The problem you might run into is you'll hit a plateau and keep repeating the same tactics because those are all you know. The secret to exponential growth is to recognize that what got you here might not get you to the next level. Hire a coach or a consultant every now and then to give you a fresh perspective and help you uncover the paths to exponential results.

SUMMARY OF THIS LESSON'S ACTION ITEMS:

- Choose an audience building channel that works for your personal strengths and preferences. Your audience building channel should feel natural and enjoyable to you.
- Formulate a basic plan to create content and grow your audience. This plan should include a rough idea for what your first pilot concept will be, how you will create the content, and of course, when you plan to make it all happen.

TIP:

If you ever get the feeling of imposter syndrome, remember this simple truth:

It's not about you, it's about the value you share.

As you begin to build an audience, you might get stage fright or feel that you're not ready. Trust me, everyone feels that at the beginning. Unfortunately, the audience doesn't care. The audience only cares about learning the story you plan to share with them. Don't worry about how you look or sound. Simply keep your chin up, stay consistent, and keep going. You will undoubtedly get better and more confident as you keep getting experience.

Your story and your wisdom are worth sharing. Don't doubt yourself!

LESSON 29:
COURSE CORRECTING TOWARDS SUCCESS

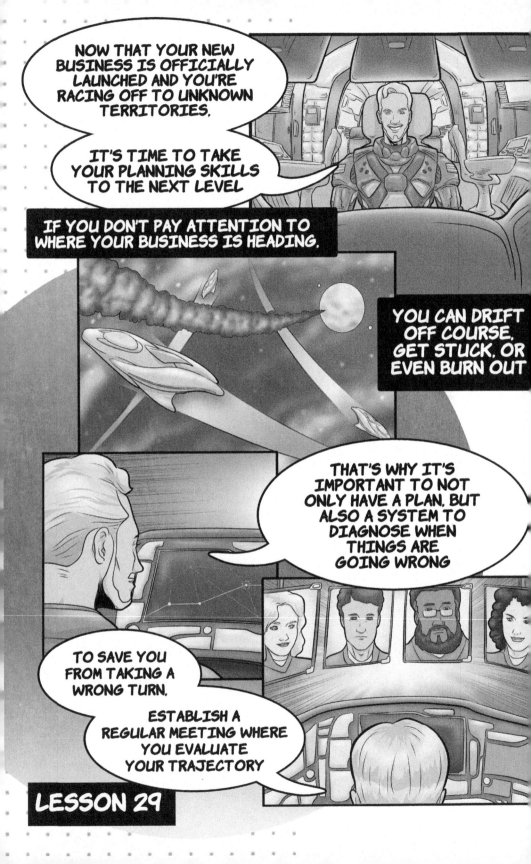

LESSON 29

LESSON 29 DETAILS

TIMELINE: DAY 35–36
ESTIMATED TIME TO COMPLETE: 40 MIN.

There's a learning curve in business. If you continue to make iterations and course corrections in the relentless growth of your business, you'll eventually cross a threshold to a place where everything just works. Our goal in this lesson is to shorten the amount of time you spend in that learning curve through implementing regular reflection on your business processes and results.

More often than not, solutions and strategies already exist for whatever challenge you are facing. These solutions are often right under our nose.

Unfortunately, if we don't have a process for actively questioning whether we're doing the right things, we might not ever ask for the solution to appear. And so, we keep on doing whatever we have been doing, oblivious that there was ever a better way. It's the simple challenge of not knowing what we don't know.

Over time, these small deviations from the intended direction of your business will start to stack up, and will make it very difficult to get back on track. You want to create a habit for steadily monitoring your direction, scanning for threats or shortcuts, and steering your business in the right direction.

Here's a simple three part program to bake into your monthly business task list that should help you identify roadblocks and choose solutions that have the best odds of success.

Step 1: Identify Roadblocks, Issues and Opportunities

Your car has indicator lights that pop up on the dashboard whenever something is not performing as it should. If you ignore these lights and just keep driving, eventually you'll run into some major complications, and possibly break your car beyond repair.

It's important to run similar diagnostic checks on the health of your business to prevent unexpected complications in the future. Eventually, you can build scorecards and tracking systems that can monitor the health of your business automatically behind the scenes, but at this stage, we'll simply run a manual diagnosis once a month.

Each month, take 30 to 60 minutes to sit down and list all the things that could possibly go wrong (or are already going wrong). This is also called an inversion exercise, or a threats analysis. You can sort through these threats or issues and prioritize them by the likeliness to happen and the severity of impact. Take the issues that require the most immediate attention and bring them to the next stage. For fun, you can also do this exercise focused on opportunities instead of issues.

Step 2: Propose Solutions Based on Your Past Wins (or Your Competition's Wins)

For each issue, you can look for solutions based on adapting things that have worked well for you in the past, or by adopting some strategies your competition has been deploying. The goal here is to spend more time deploying solutions that work, and less time throwing spaghetti at the wall.

If you discover a solution that will have a major impact on solving the issue, and you have high confidence that it will work because similar solutions have worked in the past, and it's very easy to deploy because you can delegate to a talented contractor, then you would prioritize that solution over one that might be challenging to execute or unlikely to produce positive results.

Break your solutions up into actionable steps and assign them to the people involved. I typically use Asana for all of this. Keep track of the results and bring them into the next step.

Step 3: Evaluate the Results and Double Down on Winners

In your subsequent diagnostics meetings, you should set aside some time to look at the results of the solutions you executed on from previous meetings. If something worked in the past, you can then lock it into your future processes and have it become the go-to solution any time this issue pops up. Every time you find a winner, document it in your businesses wiki, FAQ, or process manual.

If you do this consistently enough, you'll discover one day where things are just running like a well oiled machine and you're able to take yourself out of the day-to-day. It's a long slog, and the work is never really done. But the feeling of accomplishment you'll achieve through steadily solving obstacles will be an amazing reward well worth the effort.

Every minor course correction you make will get you closer and closer to finding that sweet spot of getting your business "right." If there's anything you should take away from this lesson it's this: don't neglect maintenance in your business. Establish and follow a regular cadence to monitor, diagnose, and adjust the gears that drive your business.

SUMMARY OF THIS LESSON'S ACTION ITEMS:

- Schedule a recurring weekly meeting to run through diagnostic checks on the obstacles and issues in your business and come up with solutions.
- Create an agenda for your weekly meetings. This agenda should have the same format each week and should have time set aside for discussing obstacles as well as time for assigning tasks related to the solutions.
- Create a spreadsheet, document, or other simple format to collect new obstacles that pop up during the week. You'll also want to keep this document handy during the meeting so you can jot down the solutions discussed next to each obstacle.

TIP:

I once read a workshop idea in Jeremy Gutsche's book Create the Future that can be another great format to emulate when creating your meeting agenda. Jeremy's concept was fairly simple: imagine the possible futures of your business as a utopia (raging success), and as an utter failure. What would have to happen for your business to land in either category?

The exercise goes on to instruct you to choose the biggest three contributors to each possible future and list those as priorities. These are the big things that would have to happen for you to create utopia or disaster. You can also call those your 90 day goals, your key performance indicators (KPIs), or your core missions. I personally like calling these priorities 'missions' because it gives me the feeling of solving a quest in a video game.

After you set your priorities or core missions, you'll come up with some simple long term strategies and short term tactics to achieve them. Often, without having the big picture, it becomes easy to chase symptoms in the business and preoccupy yourself with busy work. Tying your short term tactics and solutions to larger strategies related to your core mission will keep you on track and focused on solving things related to progress, not busyness.

You can download a template of this big picture worksheet on the resources section of my website.

RAGING SUCCESS	TOTAL DISASTER
Core Missions	**Core Missions**
Long Term Strategy (to achieve core missions)	**Long Term Strategy** (to achieve core missions)
Short Term Tactics (to achieve strategies above)	**Short Term Tactics** (to achieve strategies above)

LESSON 30:
EYES ON THE PRIZE

THE NUMBER ONE CHALLENGE YOU'RE GOING TO COME ACROSS IN GROWING YOUR BUSINESS IS DISTRACTION.

THE COURAGE AND DISCIPLINE TO STAY FOCUSED AMIDST ALL THE SHINY OBJECTS YOU COME ACROSS...

...WILL BECOME YOUR GREATEST TREAS[U...]

THIS FOCUS WILL SAVE YOU MONTHS, IF NOT YEARS, OF WASTED EFFORT, BURNOUT, OR JUST OVEREXTENDING YOURSELF.

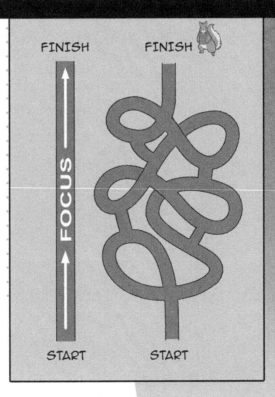

SO SLOW DOWN, TAKE THINGS ONE AT A TIME.

YOUR MISSION N THIS LESSON IS TO LOOK AT ALL THE PROJECTS YOU HAVE AVAILABLE IN YOUR BUSINESS AND CHOOSE THE ONE THAT YOU WILL GIVE YOUR FULL FOCUS.

AND REMEMBER TO CELEBRATE YOUR PROGRESS ALONG THE WAY.

BREAK THAT PROJECT UP INTO ACTIONABLE 30, 60 AND 90 DAY GOALS

THEN, CARVE OUT TIME IN YOUR CALENDAR TO WORK ON THOSE SPECIFIC GOALS BY REMOVING 'DEAD WEIGHT TASKS' THAT GET IN THE WAY OF YOUR PROGRESS.

LESSON 30 DETAILS

It's no secret that we live in a highly distracting world. ADHD is no joke. Entrepreneurs and side-hustlers are notorious for spinning so many projects at once at the detriment to their health, relationships, and even to their beloved projects.

But there's a method to harness your inner squirrel and turn that ADHD into a superpower: Merciless Focus.

The reason I call it 'merciless' is because you truly must show no mercy to your distractions. You will be endlessly tempted to take on one more side project, one more cheap client, one more half finished product launch, one more incredible opportunity... one more straw on the camel's back. Do not listen to the Siren's call. Do not give in to the allure of one more project to add to your already full plate. Keep your eyes on the prize and show no mercy to your distractions.

You will always have time to take on new projects as soon as you finish launching your current initiative and have properly set it up for a smooth run.

Merciless Focus is composed of two core principles.

The first principle is that every new project will either bring you closer to your target goal, or derail you from your target path and send you in a different direction. You must evaluate every new project or opportunity against this principle. If the project isn't directly related to advancing your target goal, show no mercy and either delete it from your wish list entirely, or delay it until you have the available resources to pursue it without impacting your primary objective.

Merciless Focus narrows the possibility for getting sidetracked by using a rock solid decision making process that sets clear, achievable project goals directly correlated to your larger business mission. The way this works is simple. Just like at the beginning of the book when you chose to launch ONE business idea and discard the others, you can deploy the same method to the direction your business is taking. If you are contemplating launching an additional service, or adding a new flavor to your menu, wait until your existing products or services are running like a well oiled machine, THEN you can start to add on more complexity.

The second principle is simple: don't bite off more than you can chew. If you don't have the capacity to take on a project, even if it might be related to your primary objective, delay it. It's always good to push yourself a little beyond your comfort zone, and to challenge yourself to complete a big initiative, but if that challenge comes at the expense of all the wheels falling off of your machine and your entire operation buckling under the pressure, is it worth it? Absolutely not.

Use a scheduling and calendar process to filter emergent tasks and schedule them off to a distant future or delegate them out. This calendar system should also allow time for distractions so that they don't creep in to your execution time.

As you grow your business, you're going to constantly be pulled into many directions. Here are some tips and strategies that can help to keep you from losing sight of what's important. Remember, distractions don't only come in the form of side projects, they can also be bad habits or self doubt.

Set Milestones

Break up a project into smaller pieces and then schedule them out across a series of weeks. You can have certain milestones to aim for each month, then distribute the tasks that make up each milestone across each week.

Celebrate Your Progress

You might feel pressure to always achieve more as you wake up each day looking at your to-do list. You might find yourself comparing yourself to others, whether competitors, friends or strangers. In times like these, it's important to validate yourself. Remind yourself of the incredible progress you've made so far. Remember that you are right where you're supposed to be, and this is an adventure.

Take things one at a time, reward the small victories and above all, congratulate yourself on how much you are learning and growing along the way. When it feels like you need to be a little more disciplined with your progress, try giving yourself just 20 to 30 minutes a day to chip away at your most important project in the morning. This will keep you feeling like you have the momentum and keep you from breaking the chain on making progress towards your number one goal if you're spread thin.

Drop the Dead Weight

Take inventory of your daily life. You've probably picked up a lot of dead weight along your life that might be things like random unconscious habits, over indulgences, unnecessary commitments to friends and family, or unnecessary hobbies (or things that can be placed on pause while you plow through this next milestone).

For each item on the inventory list of your daily life you can make some very simple decisions. First, next to each item, write how long you spend doing it. Then, decide if this action increases your progress towards your current project objective or distracts you from making progress. If it's not related to your current project, you guessed it, consider cutting it out.

As you're working on cutting out dead weight it's important to remember that it works the other way around too. If you push yourself too hard and only focus on work, your body will wear out and you'll become much less productive in the end. So, double down and do more of the things that help you get more energy and build mental clarity. Good activities to include in this list are: exercise, sleep, meditation, and time to read and think.

Putting It All Together

All that being said, Merciless Focus doesn't mean you should shame yourself if you let a few things slip through the cracks. It's important to note: DO NOT GET HARD ON YOURSELF here if you can't break all of your distractions at once. Remember, these habits have become a part of your daily routine for years, gradually. We're slowly removing them, one at a time. This is the same as course correcting. You're going to relapse here and there, and that's okay. What's important is that you keep getting back up, and you keep making adjustments to these habits until you let the distractions go completely.

As you start to run your business, you'll be presented with an endless stream of choices and shiny objects. Keep things simple, and every time you are faced with a decision that will take up your time and energy, ask yourself simply, "Will this help me get closer to my main objective, and do I need to handle it now?" If you can delegate the task or set it to be accomplished later, that will do wonders in keeping you present and focused on the current project.

SUMMARY OF THIS LESSON'S ACTION ITEMS:

- Take your next project and break it down into sprints and milestones. What are the 30, 60 and 90 day goals? What are the individual tasks that would need to happen across each week of the project? You can download the template for filling out a project based on this format at the end of the lesson.
- Create a list of your 'dead weight' tasks and make a plan to drop them out of your life. Are there things you're spending time on now that are pulling you away from your goals? Use the template below to document these goals and make a commitment to eliminate or pause them until you finish your next project.

TIP:

Using a goal tracking planner can help you stay on target. There are plenty of fantastic planners out there that you can use to track your progress and build a habit of writing your daily reflections. (I may even release my own project launch planner in the months after this book is published if there's enough interest.)

If you don't have access to a planner, you can download the goal setting worksheets in the resources section of my website. Get in the habit of journaling your progress daily and when you stop to look back, you'll be amazed at how far you've progressed.

LESSON 31:
THE POWER OF
COMMUNITY

LESSON 31 DETAILS

Sure, the lone wolf maverick entrepreneur who single-handedly builds a billion dollar company against all odds is sometimes glamorized in fictional TV and gossip magazines, but the reality is, nearly all great business owners develop greatness through cultivating their relationships.

Just like I encouraged you to *lean out* of habits that aren't complimentary to your success, now it's time to *lean* in towards a community that will help propel you forward. Networking can be intimidating for a lot of people. Most people are not wired to be "power connectors" who can find business deals and connect powerful individuals on a regular basis.

That is a skill that can take many years to cultivate. But that doesn't mean you should give up entirely on building a powerful business community to support you. There are, in fact, many ways to build a community no matter how introverted you are.

To get an idea of how community can support you as you embark on your business venture, here are a few benefits:

- Peer support and motivation
- Faster learning

- Shared resources
- Competitive accountability
- Access to more referrals and opportunities

Throughout the book, I've alluded to the power of your network in helping you close sales, troubleshoot problems and expand your audience. There's another aspect of community that shouldn't be glossed over: collective learning. When you're interacting with like minded peers on a regular basis, you'll be able to share strategies and tactics to help each other sidestep mistakes and shorten the learning curve together.

You'll also be able to pool resources and talent. When searching for a new graphic designer or web developer, you can spend days scanning portfolios and checking references if you did it on your own. But imagine having a trusted peer who has already vetted a team of talent that you could ask for recommendations. Everything is easier when you have a community.

Okay great, but how do you go about actually cultivating this magical thing called community? There are fundamentally four ways to meet new people and expand your circle:

1. **Join an existing community or mastermind.**

   - This method is easy, and works fast. A mastermind is a group of individuals coming together to help each other out and provide connections, similar to a social club. The challenge is these groups can become very expensive and might not be suited for beginners. There are certainly free communities, but a free membership might not come with the same curated value as a premium group.

2. **Meet people through calculated outreach, referrals, and schmoozing.**

   - This method has potential for very impactful partnerships. You'll need plenty of strategic practice to get it working, but with the right effort you can forge game changing connections. Additionally, you'll need thick skin and a relentless follow up process. I'm not suited for this style, so I hire assistants who excel with this approach.

3. **Attract people as a thought leader with highly visible marketing.**

    - This method takes time to build, but can be very powerful in the long run. This method might also encompass building an audience or creating your own mastermind group or networking event.

4. **Double down on luck, chance, and synchronicity.**

    - As woo as it sounds, you're more than capable of creating luck. Luck comes when you relentlessly put yourself out there. You'll find this method starts to occur consistently when you exhibit a deep passion for whatever you are doing. People are drawn to passion and motivation. If you're consistently present and showing up excited about your projects every day, you will undoubtedly meet people who will want to help you out.

If you're looking to get started right away, one of the fastest ways to meet like minded peers who are *also* looking for the same thing is to join an existing network. There are many networks out there, below is a list to get you some ideas of where you might look.

- Friends and family
- Mentors
- Peers / colleagues
- Organized networking groups (BMI, Chamber of Commerce)
- Premium masterminds (EO, YPO)
- Thought leader fan communities (Facebook groups, Discord groups, etc.)
- Conferences
- Informal masterminds (loosely gathered friends)
- Local meetups / support groups

SUMMARY OF THIS LESSON'S ACTION ITEMS:

- Research and join a support group or networking community. Choose a community that suits your needs and your budget. You're going to have a much greater chance of long term success if you join a community, so don't put this off. You don't need to be active in numerous communities. Choose one or two to focus on and down the road you can add additional networking strategies once you're up and rolling.
- Make a plan for regularly improving your networking or community interaction. If you've chosen to go down the path of direct outreach, this might be the number of people you plan to contact each week. If you're joining an existing group, it might be how many posts or meetings you'll contribute to each week.

TIP:

If you're looking for something specifically catered to new business owners starting and growing a side hustle, there's a community right at your fingertips. At the time of writing this, I'm creating a digital community that connects you with people who are going through the program just like you. You can join by visiting www.startbrigade.com and filling out an application.

As I have been growing so many of my previous businesses and side hustles, I've always yearned for a community of like minded peers that wasn't filled with elitist machismo BS. The problem I see with most mastermind programs is the elite price tag. These programs are wonderful for 7 or 8 figure businesses, but there really aren't enough well structured and value driven programs for early stage entrepreneurs and side hustlers. So as my mission to help champion prosperity for new entrepreneurs, I've created a group that focuses on peer support, competition, and collective learning.

You can sign up for the mastermind on my website. You can enroll monthly and get instant access to a library of templates and swipe files, productivity guides, more illustrations, and a step-by-step walk through of the launch plan discussed in this book. Best of all, you'll be connected to other business owners at all stages. The community starts as you launch your business and continues through as you begin to scale and automate your business.

I don't want you to feel like you're alone in this. Your side hustle should be fun, fulfilling, and financially rewarding. The community will keep you accountable so that you can move forward with confidence. So, take the time now to visit my website and sign up to the members academy.

LESSON 32: ONWARDS AND UPWARDS

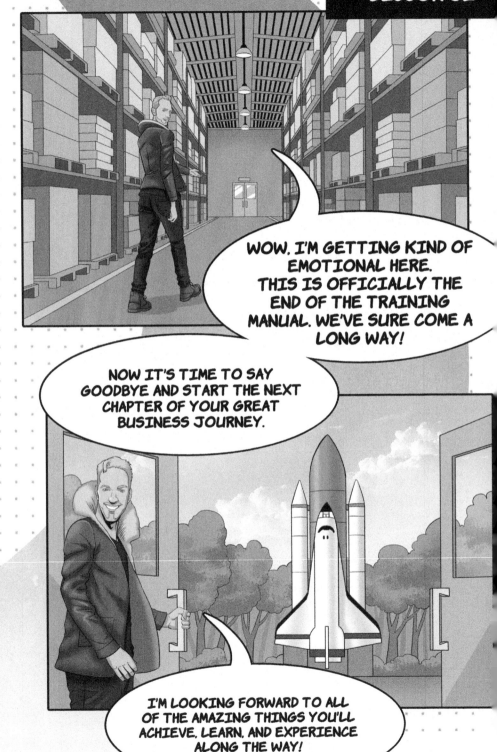

LESSON 32 DETAILS

We've reached the final chapter of this book, but it's also the first step on your new journey as a full fledged side hustler. I want to sincerely congratulate you on making it this far in the journey.

Building a business is never easy, especially if it's the first or second time you're doing it. Take a minute to pat yourself on the back for coming this far. You have built an incredible infrastructure that wasn't in place before. By going through the exercises in this book, you've developed a new skill set, you've built a sales machine, and you've created a system for launching a new revenue stream.

Now you have the wonderful opportunity to continue building this income stream to a powerful river that can give you the freedom to contribute to all the causes and projects you desire. Or, if after you've built your new side hustle, you've discovered that it's not something you would like to continue for the long run, you get to take all the new knowledge, skills, templates, systems, connections, and team members that you've built while growing this project and apply them to your next one.

The learning curve will be faster, the rate in which you can go from zero to profit will be faster and more predictable. In short, you're becoming a launch master. Keep putting in the reps, keep expanding your knowledge. You'll be surprised at how fast you can launch your next project after going through everything with your first launch.

Ultimately, it is my hope that you can use your first business as a cash generating platform from which you can launch all kinds of new endeavors. The goal is to get your first business running by itself so that you can be free to explore the next opportunity.

Of course, if you absolutely love the craft of your side hustle and would prefer to continue to develop a deep mastery within this specific business, by all means, go for it.

This is just the beginning. You have an exciting, incredible journey ahead of you and I'm delighted that this book could be a part of helping you get started. If you found value in this book, please share it with others so that they can pick up the torch and continue to pioneer new and exciting ideas that can change the world.

The reality is our planet needs creative, change-minded people to rise up, unlock their full potential and cut the tethers of poverty and limited thinking. We absolutely must find a way to keep our creative minds funded so that we can steer the planet toward a more sustainable and prosperous future. I firmly believe that you, the powerful future leaders who are reading this book, will do incredible things.

If you ever get stuck along the way, please reach out to me through my website www.startbrigade.com and I will help identify a way to break through your plateau and get you well on the way to launching a fantastic side hustle that you can rely on for years to come.

It's been an incredible adventure. Thank you for joining me.

Made in the USA
Coppell, TX
17 November 2021